The Just War Revisited

Leading political theologian Oliver O'Donovan here takes a fresh look at some traditional moral arguments about war. Modern Christians differ widely on this issue. A few hold that absolute pacifism is the only viable Christian position, others subscribe in various ways to concepts of 'just war' developed out of a Western tradition that arose from the legacies of Augustine and Aquinas, while others again adopt more pragmatically realist postures. But what bearing does theology have on the issue, and is any kind of moral consensus possible?

Professor O'Donovan tackles the problem in a manner familiar from his earlier landmark volume *The Desire of the Nations*. He argues that since the Reformation the development of religious positions cannot be dissociated from the rise of legal theory and secular forms of justice. At the heart of the issue must lie a proper understanding of the relationship between politics and theology; and our sources are as likely to be Grotius or Locke as more overtly theological thinkers. In this light, O'Donovan re-examines questions of contemporary urgency including the use of biological and nuclear weapons, military intervention, economic sanctions, war-crimes trials, and the roles of the Geneva Convention, international conventions, and the UN. His enquiry opens with a challenging dedication to the new Archbishop of Canterbury and proceeds to shed new light on vital topics with which that Archbishop and others will be very directly engaged. It should be read by anyone concerned with the ethics of warfare.

OLIVER O'DONOVAN is Regius Professor of Moral and Pastoral Theology and Canon of Christ Church, University of Oxford. He is the author of *The Problem of Self-Love in Saint Augustine* (1980), *Begotten or Made* (1984), *The Desire of the Nations* (1996), *Peace and Certainty: A Theological Essay on Deterrence* (1989), *On the Thirty-Nine Articles: A Conversation with Tudor Christianity* (1993), *Resurrection and Moral Order* (1986), and *Common Objects of Love* (2002).

CURRENT ISSUES IN THEOLOGY

General Editor

Iain Torrance

Professor in Patristics and Christian Ethics, Master of Christ's College, and Dean of the Faculty of Arts and *Divinity, University of Aberdeen*

Editorial Advisory Board

David Ford *University of Cambridge*
Bryan Spinks *Yale University*
Kathryn Tanner *University of Chicago*
John Webster *University of Aberdeen*

There is a need among upper-undergraduate and graduate students of theology, as well as among Christian teachers and church professionals, for a series of short, focussed studies of particular key topics in theology written by prominent theologians. *Current Issues in Theology* meets this need.

The books in the series are designed to provide a 'state-of-the-art' statement on the topic in question, engaging with contemporary thinking as well as providing original insights. The aim is to publish books which stand between the static monograph genre and the more immediate statement of a journal article, by authors who are questioning existing paradigms or rethinking perspectives.

Other titles in the series:

Holy Scripture: A Dogmatic Sketch John Webster

The Just War Revisited

OLIVER O'DONOVAN

CAMBRIDGE
UNIVERSITY PRESS

PUBLISHED BY THE PRESS SYNDICATE OF THE UNIVERSITY OF CAMBRIDGE
The Pitt Building, Trumpington Street, Cambridge, United Kingdom

CAMBRIDGE UNIVERSITY PRESS
The Edinburgh Building, Cambridge, CB2 2RU, UK
40 West 20th Street, New York, NY 10011–4211, USA
477 Williamstown Road, Port Melbourne, VIC 3207, Australia
Ruiz de Alarcón 13, 28014 Madrid, Spain
Dock House, The Waterfront, Cape Town 8001, South Africa

http://www.cambridge.org

First published 2003

Printed in the United Kingdom at the University Press, Cambridge

Typeface Minion 10.5/14 pt.   *System* LaTeX 2ε   [TB]

A catalogue record for this book is available from the British Library

Library of Congress Cataloguing in Publication data
O'Donovan, Oliver.
The just war revisited / by Oliver O'Donovan.
    p.   cm. – (Current issues in theology ; v. 2)
Includes bibliographical references and index.
ISBN 0 521 83138 5 – ISBN 0 521 53899 8 (pbk.)
1. War – Religious aspects – Christianity.   I. Title.   II. Series.
BT736.2.O365   2003   241'.6242–dc21

ISBN 0 521 83138 5 hardback
ISBN 0 521 53899 8 paperback

Contents

Dedicatory preface

To the Most Reverend Rowan Williams, Archbishop of Canterbury:
Dear Rowan:

In your carefree professorial days, before you were summoned home to your pastoral responsibilities in Wales, you and I found ourselves pursuing a friendly disagreement over the Gulf War of 1991 in front of a politely detached audience of colleagues and students. That modest occasion was recalled by Kenneth W. Vaux, in the introduction to his own contribution to the same discussion, where he generously wrote that we 'framed the debate with boldness and courage and stimulated a lively and respectful dialogue, not only in the university but in the wider church and society'.[1] Did we, indeed? I recognise our intention, well enough, but for two professors to have such an edifying effect on the wider church and society would have been something of a phenomenon. But now God has placed you in a position where, for better or worse, anything you say can be relied on to excite a lively, if not always respectful, response within the wider church and society. Those of us who still enjoy our professorial freedom are bound to offer you, and those who share with you the pastoral care of the church, such assistance as we can.

There are three elements in what follows, in somewhat contrasted styles. The title 'Just War Revisited' belongs to four lectures delivered in the University of Aberdeen in December 2001 under the auspices of that distinguished journal, *The Scottish Journal of Theology*, at

[1] Kenneth L. Vaux, *Ethics and the Gulf War: religion, rhetoric and righteousness.* Boulder etc., Westview Press, 1992, p. vii.

the kind invitation of the Rev. Professor Iain Torrance, Dean of the Faculty of Arts at Aberdeen and Editor of *SJT*. They aim to present, in a form which I believe to be more coherent than the bare lists of principles that usually substitute for an exposition, a longstanding tradition of thinking about war with deep roots in Christian theology. That this tradition is in fact neither a 'theory', nor about 'just wars', but *a proposal for doing justice in the theatre of war*, is a point that the reader is asked to reflect on. But pedantry will get us nowhere. As the 'just war theory' it is known to our contemporaries, and as 'just war theory' it is likely to go on being known.

Supplementing these lectures are four further short papers, one of which has seen the light of day elsewhere, the other three appearing now for the first time. These aim to address some special practical questions that have vexed the Western world in recent years, and to show how the resources of the tradition may be called on in approaching them. With these I run the risk that theologians always run in the face of complex practical questions, especially those with legal implications, that of being insufficiently versed in the details to satisfy the experts and of being too interested in them to satisfy a general readership. However, a bridge-builder can only sink half his foundations on either bank of the river. I think you will understand, with your own concerns for theology's bridge-building rôle, why I have thought this risk worth taking.

In conclusion I have added an Afterword about the international crisis we have been living through in the autumn of 2002. I did not wish to introduce this perspective into the earlier discussions, where the argument is the clearer from not being tied too closely to a particular occasion. On the other hand it seemed impossible to put a book on this subject in print at this time without some hint as to how its approach to the question might help us now. It is written, and entitled, 'without authority', to mark the difference between outlining a principled approach, on which I certainly claim *some* authority, and interpreting actual events, in which I am as open to misjudgments as anyone. The moralist knows, or ought to, that there is nothing more difficult and more perilous than reading the situation within which one actually stands.

In writing of just war 'revisited', I may arouse an expectation of something conservative, not politically but intellectually, an attempt to reinstate a tradition rather than push back its boundaries. Broadly speaking, and despite such attempts at boundary-pushing that the shorter essays undertake, this expectation is correct. No one can write on the morality of war at present without being aware of at least one frontier waiting to be opened up: a serious comparison between the Christian approach to the subject and the very different but equally careful approach of Islam. To those who have given us some preliminary guidance on the topic, I am grateful. But I have not pursued this line of enquiry here, because – well, to put it bluntly, I am not sure that a Western Christian public has *deserved* the indulgence of having two just-war theories put at its disposal, when it is clearly at a loss to know what to do with one. The attempt to understand where the West has come from must surely precede any fruitful thought of engagement.

The just-war theory of these pages is a twentieth-century recovery of an approach that had reached a considerable level of sophistication in the sixteenth and early seventeenth centuries before falling into a long disuse. Though respectable authorities have been misled on the point, it is not the 'traditional' belief of Christendom, if by 'traditional' is meant 'uninterrupted'; the dominant modes of thought both in the early patristic period and in the eighteenth and nineteenth centuries were different, though in contrary ways. The stimulus to its recovery came from the Hague Conventions, and the moral urgency that accompanied it was provided by the agenda of the pseudo-heroic 'stategic air war' and its ugly, pouting grandchild, 'massive nuclear deterrence'. With the shift of geopolitical attention that accompanied the end of the cold war, the just war contention, together with the deterrence controversy, fell victim to a certain lapse of memory, and that is what provokes an attempt to 'revisit' it, not least because failure to recall the moral tradition is accompanied by failure to recall important events, even very recent ones. Not only 'theory' but 'experience', too, eludes us as we try to comprehend the highly threatening international landscape of our new century and to conceive ways of travelling safely and charitably across it.

Running through the discussion is a recurrent reflection: citizens of democracies do not know how to adopt a posture of *practical reasonableness* in the face of large challenges to peace. I have written below of the 'spirituality' of the just-war theory, by which is meant its capacity to make the reflecting subject conscious of his or her own responsible position before God in relation to other members of society who have their own differently responsible positions. The decisions are, on the one hand, *ours*, and not to be thrown off on to others' shoulders with a shudder of irritated editorialising; yet they are not ours *exclusively*, but only in relation to, and with respect for, politically responsible deciders, among whom we have to learn to deliberate sympathetically and collaboratively. If it is the case, as I suspect it is, that the reason the classic just-war theorists were good at inculcating this posture of responsibility was precisely that they believed in God's sovereignty and the world's redemption, one may expect to find it nourished especially in the discourse of the Christian churches.

There, however, one is too frequently disappointed. One of the considerations that moves me to commit these thoughts on armed conflict to print at this point is that those to whom it falls to guide Christian reflections in a time of war and rumours of war seem to have difficulty in taking the measure of their task. For this reason I address this little book to you, a friend on whom the heaviest of such burdens has come to rest. Not that you need me to supply you with ideas on the subject. But I dare to hope that in the reflections that follow, whether they persuade you or not, iron may sharpen iron, putting a suitable edge on your thoughts for the service of the church and the political community.

Advent 2002

1 | Just war revisited

1 Antagonistic praxis and evangelical counter-praxis

On the famous Ghent altarpiece, on which the Van Eyck brothers depicted the adoration of the Lamb of God standing upon an altar on a greensward in front of the Heavenly Jerusalem, there appear in the lower left-hand panel two groups of people at the edge of the worshipping crowd. They are separated from each other by a rocky outcrop, but share a common urban background; and that contrasts them with a balancing pair of groups on the lower right-hand panel, set against a wilderness landscape. Those on the right are the hermits and the pilgrims of the church; but the groups on the left are identified as the church's just judges and *milites Christi*, 'soldiers of Christ'. To our modern sensibilities this is immediately shocking. How, we wonder, could the lay service exercised in a civil context by Christian judges come to be extended to soldiers? The one group serves peace, the other war; this seems enough to set an infinite spiritual distance between them. Can one who fights offer worship to the sacrificed Lamb? Our sense of shock is excusable. Yet the idea that these two roles, judges and soldiers, are analogous, an idea that grew out of the twelfth-century romanticisation of the Christian knight such as we meet in the legends of the Round Table, was one of the great achievements of the late middle ages. Today we commonly call it the 'just war theory'.

There are good reasons to hesitate over this achievement. The will of God for humankind is peace: that all-determining truth contains, and shapes, any further truths that we may hope to learn on this subject. And from it flow three further propositions. First, God's peace is the original *ontological* truth of creation. We must deny the sceptical proposition that competition and what metaphysicians call 'difference' are the fundamental realities of the universe, a proposition which the creation, preservation and redemption of the world make impossible to entertain. Secondly, God's peace is the goal of *history*. We must deny the supposed cultural value of war, its heroic glorification as an advancement of civilisation. For war serves the ends of history only as evil serves good, and the power to bring good out of evil belongs to God alone. Thirdly, God's peace is a *practical demand* laid upon us. We must deny any 'right' to the pursuit of war, any claim on the part of a people that it may sacrifice its neighbours in the cause of its own survival or prosperity. For the Gospel demands that we renounce goods that can only be won at the cost of our neighbours' good.

Philologically, *bellum* is *duellum*, the confrontation of two, the simple and unmediated difference of opposites. No Christian believes that *duellum* can be 'just' or 'necessary', because no Christian believes that opposition can in fact be unmediated. All oppositions are subject to the pacific judgment of God, of which neither party is independent. To this extent every Christian is, to use a term which had some currency early in the twentieth century, a 'pacificist', rejecting antagonistic praxis, the praxis of unmediated conflict. All Christians, therefore, can recognise something like a sin of belligerence or a 'crime against peace'. That crime consists in making antagonistic praxis a goal of politics, whether as means or end; that sin consists in cultivating antagonism as a form of self-perfection.

Against what moral standard is war a crime or a sin? Here, indeed, is a puzzle. For there is universal evidence of a connection between warlike behaviour and the development of culture. Antagonistic praxis is strongly tied to the cultivation of certain human virtues; it is the occasion of achievement, self-discipline and virtuosity. This is made possible by a psychological fact, that the peril of confrontation with a mortal enemy may evoke a sudden access of courage and capacity. Within his interpretation of the human passions, St Thomas spoke of what he called an 'irascible contrariety', by which he meant that our passionate reactions to good and evil not only take the form of an instinctive attraction and repulsion, but also, as we see good and evil as presenting a challenge to our own capacities, of a reflective contrary movement, shrinking from or pressing towards action.[1] So faced with an immediate threat to our lives, there is released within us a dialectical response, not only of extreme fear but of extreme boldness, on the basis of which a culture of the virtue of courage may be perfected.

From Achilles to Patton, war offers its rich and varied crop of military heroes, for whom the destruction of enemies has been the stuff of outstanding performance, whether in brutal hand-to-hand assault or in elegant tactical ingenuity. But the satisfaction of disposing of an enemy is not confined to the hero himself, nor even to those who fight alongside him and aspire to imitate him. The hero is, in fact, never as solitary as the songs that celebrate him make him seem. His combat is a moment in the building of a society; his enterprise furthers the life of a community of men, women and children, for whom the warrior's deeds are a common point of reference, a 'transcendental representation', and who reinforce with passionate self-censure the narrowed moral perspectives which pave the way for heroic virtues. The unbridled excess of war, the ritual mutilation of corpses, the slaughter of non-combatants, the rape of women, the destruction of property, every kind of violent display, in fact, are all indivisibly of a piece with its constructive, culture-building and virtue-perfecting aspects. They are the rituals through which the mortal conflict of a few becomes the common object of love within a political society.

Furthermore, the access of heroic courage is surrounded by a wealth of disciplines and restraints. The practical traditions of the

---

[1] St Thomas Aquinas, *Summa Theologiae* 1–2.23.2. Blackfriars edn, ed. Thomas R. Heath, vol. xxxv, London, Eyre and Spottiswoode and New York, McGraw Hill, 1972, pp. 80–5; also in Oliver O'Donovan and Joan Lockwood O'Donovan, eds, *From Irenaeus to Grotius*, Grand Rapids, Eerdmans, 1999 (hereafter *IG*), p. 354.

warrior classes, found in many cultures, develop virtues of self-mastery, decisive action and contempt for death, creating an élite to which the combatant rôle is confined. In Israel's traditions, on the other hand, which were comparatively inhospitable to heroic ideals and jealous of the popular militia, a different set of disciplines emerges, sometimes clashing with the heroic ones.[2] Cultic restraints surrounding warfare present a theological interpretation of battle as a moment of special divine empowerment. Religious law forbids committal to battle without the assurance of prophecy and oracle that the cause is YHWH's own, since such engagements are not available for the pursuit of ordinary human goals, and the temptations of self-enrichment must be offset by a general destruction. In their different ways these two traditions of restraint have a similar aim: to construct a wall around the encounter of battle, to make an unbridgeable difference between the ordinary relations which bind peoples to neighbouring peoples and the exceptional moment of antagonistic confrontation. The heroic ethic demands magnanimity when the critical moment is past; it forbids 'avenging in time of peace blood which had been shed in war' (1 Kings 2:5). The destructiveness of battle may not spill into the subsequent life of the community, and in the greatest celebrations of warrior deeds the heroism of the vanquished is honoured alongside that of the victors. In ancient traditions, then, antagonistic praxis is separated off. It is treated as a special and occasional eventuality, a crisis in which the ordinary rules of social recognition are dissolved in mutual bloodshed, but which in turn is decisively set aside, so that ordinary rules of social recognition may reassert themselves.

This entwining of the pursuit of war with the growth of civilisation directs us to the moment of truth in the old assertion that self-defence was a natural right. The praxis of mortal combat is not destructive to human sociality as such; it is simply a moment at which human

---

[2] 1 Sam. 14 demonstrates a clash between the cultic and heroic schools within Israel's interpretation of war. Cf. my *The Desire of the Nations*, Cambridge, Cambridge University Press, 1996, pp. 55f.

sociality regroups and renews itself. The rejection of war, then, is no demand of natural law. It is a distinctively *evangelical* rejection. Christians refused to go along with this controlled recognition of antagonistic praxis and its associated virtues. They had a message to proclaim about the end of history: the episodic collapse and recovery of sociality was something that God had done away with once for all in the cross and exaltation of Christ. The unification of all rule in his rule, the subordination of all sovereignty under his sovereignty, forbade them to think that sheer unmediated antagonism could, in however carefully defined circumstances, be admitted as a possibility. Since every opposition of hostile parties was subject to the throne of God and of his Christ, there could be no outright duality. Antagonistic praxis was superseded by the climax of salvation-history. To use the phrase of John Milbank, whose framing of the problematic we have to some degree followed, a counter-praxis was demanded, a 'peaceful transmission of difference', that would overcome the confrontation of the two with the rule of the one, revealing the unifying order of the kingdom of God.[3]

But what is the shape of this counter-praxis? It cannot be the waging of peace *against* violence. Christians believe that violence, in the radical ontological sense, 'is not'; and to oppose violence with peace is to agree that violence 'is'. The praxis which corresponds to the ontology of peace is not a praxis *of peace* simply and as such, but a praxis of winning peace out of opposition. 'Not the simple *being* of peace,' as Bernd Wannenwetsch declares, 'but the *service* of reconciliation'.[4]

---

[3] For the phrase, see John Milbank, *Theology and Social Theory*, Oxford, Blackwell, 1990, p. 417.

[4] Bernd Wannenwetsch, *Gottesdienst als Lebensform*, Stuttgart, Kohlhammer, 1997, pp. 127–9, drawing attention to Milbank's slide from a 'gigantic claim' at the ontological level into 'seemingly inescapable resignation', and seeing this correctly as the result of a conception of the church's praxis that takes violence too seriously: 'Nicht das *Wesen* des Friedens, sondern das *Amt* der Versöhnung; nicht das Wesen des *Friedens*, sondern das Amt der *Versöhnung*.'

This counter-praxis has more than one theatre. Staged against the supportive backdrop of the community of belief and worship, it takes a pastoral shape as mutual forgiveness, by which enemies who believe the Gospel are made enemies no longer. But it must also be staged missiologically against a backdrop of unbelief and disobedience, and here it assumes the secular form of judgment – not final judgment, but judgment as the interim provision of God's common grace, promising the dawning of God's final peace. This, too, is a word (not the first or last word, but an interim word) of evangelical proclamation: God has provided us a *saeculum*, a time to live, to believe and to hope under a régime of provisional judgment; here, too, it is possible to practise reconciliation, since God's patience waits, and preserves the world against its own self-destruction.

The practical content of this interim common grace is the *political act*, the same political act that we encounter in any other political context: government-as-judgment, the exercise of Gospel faith within the theatre of unbelief and disobedience. This may be exercised also in response to the crime of war. The outcome of this act of judgment, when it is successful, is like the outcome of every other successful act of judgment: a law, which regulates relations between the parties and provides the measure for their future peace. The evangelical counter-praxis to war, then, amounts to this: armed conflict can and must be re-conceived as an extraordinary extension of ordinary acts of judgment; it can and must be subject to the limits and disciplines of ordinary acts of judgment. In the face of criminal warmaking, judgment may take effect through armed conflict, but only as armed conflict is conformed to the law-governed and law-generating shape of judgment.

Materially, this proposal may appear to amount simply to another kind of war – a 'just' war. But the name by which the proposal has been universally known in the last generation – 'just-war theory' – is a misnomer, since it is not, in the first place, a 'theory', but a proposal of *practical* reason; and it is not, in the second place, about 'just wars', but about how we may enact just judgment even in the theatre of war. The term 'war' itself, subject to every kind of reification and deconstruction, is hardly usable. Formally, what is proposed is *toto caelo* different from the crime of war: it is a provisional witness to the unity of God's rule in the face of the antagonistic praxis of *duellum*. Yet it is no less true in this form than in any other that judgment has only the same material means available to it as crime. Armed conflict is the means it requires, because armed conflict is the means by which the crime of war is practised. To take up *these* means, and to convert them to the service of that law-bound and obedient judgment, was the constructive work of Christian 'poetics', an exercise of the practical imagination in service of international justice, rather than in national self-defence or self-aggrandisement.

'Pacifism' is the name usually given to one of two possible strategies – the more recognisably Christian of the two – for refusing this Christian proposal. It characteristically limits an *active* counter-praxis to within the primary, pastoral theatre, while within the secondary, missiological theatre it restricts itself to a passive counter-praxis of endurance and martyrdom. It has been popular in recent years to say that there are not one but many 'pacifisms', and for the purposes of a sociological typology this is no doubt true.[5] But for the purposes of practical reason one pacifism is enough: in the face of a praxis of unmediated opposition, it holds that an evangelical counter-praxis of judgment is not to be looked for. The disagreement here, as is rightly said, is not a disagreement about the *means* that may be used to defend peace. It concerns the *nature* of that interim worldly peace that may in fact obtain between communities and individuals without mediating institutions of government, i.e., peace among sovereign nations. Within a pacifist perspective, this peace must be a gift of God beyond the scope of any political art. We

---

[5] For the plurality of pacifisms, an idea given popularity by John Howard Yoder's *Nevertheless: the varieties and shortcomings of religious pacifism* (Scottdale, Pa. and Kitchener, Ont., Herald Press, 1971), see most recently Stanley Hauerwas, 'Explaining Christian Nonviolence', in Ken Chase and Alan Jacobs, eds, *Christian Peace in a Violent World*, Grand Rapids, Brazos, 2002.

may do much, no doubt, to earn, claim and enjoy such a gift when it is given, by 'raising lemurs, sustaining universities, having children, and, of course, playing baseball'; but when it has splintered into a thousand warring fragments, there is no political praxis by which we may pick the fragments up and reunite them.[6] Does this reflect a theological disagreement about common grace as such? Not necessarily, for the pacifist is by no means bound to deny the operation of common grace through governments and their institutionalised judgment. But it does reflect a fairly profound disagreement about the limits of the operation of common grace. A certain 'statism' is implied in the pacifist position, which will not contemplate the *improvisation* of judgment where it is not provided for within a state structure, and to that extent cannot treat international politics wholly seriously *as* politics, a God-given sphere of peaceful interaction. Here we begin to see why pacifism is a modern development. But to this we return below.

For a short period at the end of the twentieth century, when representatives of the just-war proposal and pacifism found themselves in common opposition to the Western alliance's policies of massive deterrence, it appeared to some commentators that they converged upon a 'presumption against the use of force', the difference being merely the uncompromising spirit in which pacifists maintained the presumption over against a readiness to make exceptions.[7] But this was a mere trick of the light, which involved a misreading of the just-war proposal as essentially critical in intent. If 'just war theory' had no purpose but to disprove on a case-by-case basis claims for the justice of particular wars which pacifism had ruled out *a limine*, then it could relate to pacifism like research-assistant to professor, marshalling the detailed evidence in support of the grand hypothesis. But it is not, and never was, the function of the judicial proposal to

---

[6] Stanley Hauerwas, 'Taking Time for Peace: the moral significance of the trivial', in *Christian Existence Today*, Durham, N.C., Labyrinth Press, 1988, pp. 253–66.

[7] For an extended critique of the supposed convergence, see Joseph E. Capizzi, 'On Behalf of the Neighbour', *Studies in Christian Ethics* xiv(2), 2001, 87–108.

allow or disallow historical claims. Its business was to assert a practical claim, that God's mercy and peace may and must be witnessed to in this interim of salvation-history through a praxis of judgment, even beyond the normal reach of states.

From the earliest attempts to understand how armed conflict might be compatible with Christian discipleship, the church has taken its bearings from the evangelical command of love. Augustine's famous letter to Boniface treats the obligation of military action as an obligation of love to the neighbour. St Thomas and his followers locate the discussion of war within the treatise on the virtue of charity.[8] In the context of war we find in its sharpest and most paradoxical form the thought that love can sometimes smite, and even slay. If this thought marks the parting of the ways with pacifism, it also indicates the point at which Christian thought on war is irreconcilable with the alternative strategy for refusing the judicial proposal, which is to make *survival* the final criterion of what may and may not be done. To take survival as the bottom line is to revert to the antagonistic model of mortal combat, and so inevitably to retreat from the Gospel proclamation of the universal rule of Christ and from the praxis of loving judgment. When self-defence, of state, community or individual, has the last word, paganism is restored. Precisely for this reason a Christian witness to God's peace must always be acted out against the horizon of suffering and martyrdom. Suffering and martyrdom mark the point at which the possibilities of true judgment run out within the conditions of the world. They are necessary components of Christian practical reason, because they demonstrate the vulnerability of the praxis of judgment, and so protect it from serious misunderstanding. Judgment is an undertaking always under

---

[8] Augustine, *Epistula* 189, in *IG*, pp. 133–6; also in Augustine, *Political Writings*, ed. E.M. Atkins and R.J. Dodaro, Cambridge, Cambridge University Press, 2001, pp. 214–18. Thomas Aquinas, *Summa Theologiae* 2-2.40, set within the section *de vitiis oppositis caritati* (cf. 34 prol.); Blackfriars edn pp. 80–5. Suárez's treatise on just war forms the final section of his work *De triplici virtute theologica*, the third part of which is *de caritate*.

threat within the terms of this world, always liable to be overwhelmed by violence. It cannot possibly issue a licence to avoid defeat by all possible means.

Yet the horizon on which we are called to suffer and to die rather than wrong our neighbour is not reached before we actually reach it. The possibilities of active witness to God's peace are not exhausted until we have exhausted them, which we will not have done if we have not explored them. In this context, as in all others, the duties which confront us do not *begin* with martyrdom; they *end* with it, when we have gone as far as we are permitted to go, done as much as we are permitted to do. Martyrdom is not, in fact, a strategy for *doing* anything, but a testimony to God's faithfulness when there is nothing left to do. Which is simply to say that we cannot describe the praxis of international judgment solely by pointing to the moment at which its possibilities run out. A child invited to paint a fish may begin by painting the sea, and when the paper is awash in blue, discover too late that the fish's outline needed to be sketched in first. The praxis of judgment is that of a certain type of *action*, and no account of it can be offered in words with the prefix 'non-'. Non-violence, non-resistance and all the other great watchwords of pacifism evoke a set of limits which circumscribe the possibility of action in the world. They belong to the philosophy of transcendence, the *via negativa*. They frame every Christian witness within the eschatological non-coincidence of worldly success and the triumph of God's kingdom. But they do not describe this witness.

It has often been said that the fault of pacifism lies in a progressivist eschatology, an optimistic hope that sufficiently worthy actions will transform the existing terms of this world into those of the next. This charge may have been an appropriate response to certain religious syntheses with idealist rationalism in the early twentieth century; but it is the opposite of the truth about the Christian pacifism most frequently encountered today, which tends to be preoccupied with the distinction between the two worlds and their different suppositions, unwilling to think in terms other than those of opposition. Yet when the eschatological conflict is simply imported into ethics and presented as though it were an alternative praxis, the effect is rather the same. It shortchanges the *ethical* task of describing a witness that takes form within the conditions of the world. The pathos of suffering drowns out the practical demand, the 'it may be' of Providence, that calls us to adventure.[9] Stanley Hauerwas's claim that 'Nonresistance but names the way God has chosen to redeem us' can be sustained only as long as we emphasise the *verb*.[10] 'Nonresistance' 'names' the dawning of redemption in precisely the sense that the tetragrammaton Y H W H 'names' God. That is to say, it inducts us into the theophany, but it does not prescribe the praxis of worship. 'Nonresistance' is not an ethical term. As the cross is not the sum of how Jesus 'went about doing good', so neither is the command 'follow me' exhaustively accounted for by the words: 'when you are old you will stretch out your hands, and another will gird you and carry you where you do not wish to go'.[11]

Historically the proposal for a praxis of judgment has had two phases. Loosely, we may speak of 'just-war thinking' in the late patristic and medieval periods as an undeveloped tailpiece to the church's reflections on the role of Christian emperors. Correspondingly, we may speak only loosely of early Christian 'pacifism' in the pre-Nicene period, since the question of military service was not disentangled from the general question of involvement with a hostile pagan government.[12] But in the early-modern period the proposal assumed a distinctive shape, forced upon it by the disappearance of the Roman empire and the birth of nation-states.[13] To this phase of the discussion we shall refer when we speak of the 'classic' just-war theorists. The modern Christian discussion of war and peace

---

[9] cf. 1 Sam. 14:6.

[10] Stanley Hauerwas, *With the Grain of the Universe*, London, SCM, 2002, p. 220.

[11] John 21:18f.   [12] On this see 'The Patristic Age', *IG*, pp. 1–7.

[13] The names that dominate this development are the Spanish Catholics Francisco di Vitoria (1485–1546) and Francisco Suárez (1548–1617), and the Protestant Hugo Grotius (1583–1647).

(i.e., since the sixteenth century) presupposes the pluralism of the nation-state system, a multitude of 'peoples' become aware of themselves and asserting themselves in claims to absolute sovereignty. The just-war thinkers of the classic period looked to an international Law of Nations, *ius gentium*, to provide a bulwark against nationalist absolutism. Between the earlier and the later phases, however, there is substantial continuity, for the claims of the modern nation-state replicate an older Ciceronian vision of the city constituted for eternity, making wars *aut pro fide aut pro salute*, in defence of its allies or itself.[14] The heart of the question, both in antiquity and in modernity, is how these centres of political self-complacency are to be brought to recognise the sovereignty of the reign of God.

Approaching it from this angle we avoid two common misconceptions of the just-war theory, both of them with a historicist slant. In the first place, it is often supposed that just-war theory is *descriptive of how wars used to be conducted* within Christendom, but has become outdated as the description has ceased to be valid. But the just-war proposal is not descriptive; and the demands of practical reason do not go out of date like newspapers. It was never anything other than a practical proposal for the radical correction of the praxis of war, and the extent to which its conceptions are not followed is the extent to which they have not been attended to. Various reasons could be alleged for persistent non-compliance, and a hard-nosed realist is free to say that the proposal was morally over-ambitious and therefore impracticable from the outset. (A pacifist is not free to say this!) But nothing more needs to be said about it, perhaps, than may be equally be said in relation to any of the commands of the Decalogue or the Sermon on the Mount: sinful men and women do not keep any moral commandment all the time; men and women created in God's image do not break any moral commandment all the time.

---

[14] Cicero, *de republica* 3. fr. 34, at Augustine, *City of God* 22.6.2. Ed. R.W. Dyson, Cambridge, Cambridge University Press, 1998, p. 1117.

In the second place, it is very often supposed that just-war theory undertakes *to validate or invalidate particular wars*. That would be an impossible undertaking. History knows of no just wars, as it knows of no just peoples. Major historical events cannot be justified or criticised in one mouthful; they are concatenations and agglomerations of many separate actions and many varied results. One may justify or criticise acts of statesmen, acts of generals, acts of common soldiers or of civilians, provided that one does so from the point of view of those who performed them, i.e., without moralistic hindsight; but wars as such, like most large-scale historical phenomena, present only a great question mark, a continual invitation to reflect further on which decisions were, and which were not, justified at the time and in the circumstances. Such reflective questioning has a certain inconclusiveness about it, since our judgments on past historical actors are limited, our imagination never quite sufficient to put us wholly in the actors' shoes. It is certainly not enough to devise sceptical questions about the motives of each and every actor in turn, and then to suppose we have found a short cut to a universal moral theorem: 'just wars never happen'. Practical doctrines about what *should be done* are not established by such deconstructive means. We may make use of history to warn ourselves of the dangers of self-deception, over-confidence, mass emotion, cruelty, timidity, partial sympathy, lack of foresight, indifference, etc.; yet when these warnings are all heeded, the help that practical doctrine offers is not help for historians, but for those who wish to learn *how to engage in* the praxis of judgment – to engage in it in *these* days and in *these* circumstances, where we actually find ourselves, here and now.

The task of political ethics at this point is to provide as full a general account of the reconciling praxis of judgment as may be possible. But from what point is such an account to begin? When Thomas Aquinas asked himself whether war was always sinful, his answer listed three things required in just war: the authority of a prince, a just cause, and a right intention.[15] From the point of view of modern just-war theorists this was only half of what needed to be said; and so modern textbooks, which like to outdo Thomas in the length of their lists, present as many as seven criteria for just war arranged under the two broad headings of just resort to war (*ius ad bellum*) and just conduct of war (*ius in bello*): 'authority', 'just cause', 'intention', 'last resort' and 'prospect of success' (*ius ad bellum*), 'discrimination' and 'proportion' (*ius in bello*). Such attempts to reclaim the tradition have a disconcertingly legalist feel to them, ticking off the principles, as it were, one by one. But the train of thought involved in exploring judgment in armed combat is not reducible to a list. Thomas's sixteenth-century admirers did not follow his cataloguing habit, and were wiser not to do so.

An account must flow out from the central proposal, that armed conflict is to be re-conceived as an extraordinary extension of ordinary acts of judgment. This suggests, in the first place, that conflict can be brought within the scope of the *authority* on which government may normally call, and, in the second, that it can be undertaken in such a manner as to *establish justice*. These two suggestions must direct the exploration. Every serious contributor to the classic tradition has been concerned with the scope of political authority, on the one hand, since it is the precondition for conceiving the use of armed force as a political act, and with the structure of an effective act of judgment on the other. The latter question is explored in modern discussions primarily with the aid of the two categories, 'discrimination' and 'proportion'. The logic of these two categories lies in the nature of an act of judgment, which is both retrospective and prospective, a true pronouncement on what has gone before and an effective foundation for what is to come after, an act of disclosure and of lawgiving. Within the first of these two aspects we must distinguish a moment of 'description', which represents the moral realities of the situation, and a moment of 'discrimination', reaching a decision about innocence

---

[15] Thomas Aquinas, *Summa Theologiae* 2-2.40.1; Blackfriars edn pp. 80–5.

and guilt. These three categories – description, discrimination, and foundation – contain in principle whatever needs to be said about an act of judgment, and therefore about judgment by armed force.

What, then, of the modern (not traditional) distinction between just resort to war (*ius ad bellum*) and just conduct in war (*ius in bello*)? This, in my view, is a secondary casuistic distinction, not a load-bearing one. Decisions of different scope are taken at different moments, and while this division of the subject may usefully serve to distinguish different moments, the central rule, that an act of judgment must be a truthful pronouncement on what *has been* done and an effective foundation for what *is to be* done, applies to all decisions at whatever moment they arise. It applies to the decision to go to war, to the decision to put an end to a war, and to the multitude of decisions about how to conduct a war.

This point has a bearing on what was said earlier about the 'reification' of war. I was startled years ago by the objection a friend raised to me against Britten's *War Requiem*, one of the greatest of the twentieth-century artistic anti-war protests: it seemed to her to represent war as an object of beauty. When I listen now to the final movement, the setting of Wilfred Owen's 'Strange Meeting' with the final 'Let us sleep now!' heard against the background of a liturgical *dona eis pacem*, I find the point irresistible. And is it not a characteristic emotional strategy of Western pacifism precisely to make an aesthetic icon out of war? 'The pity of war, the pity of war distilled' is, Owen thought, 'the truth untold', that always-beckoning might-have-been of life prematurely lost, the beauty for ever hovering over the horizon beyond our reach. War takes to itself the unique pathos of death, and becomes an archetypal focus of terror and fascination, outside all narratable experience and necessarily separate from social engagement. We are warned away from war as we are warned away from the sacred *adyton*, the abode of the shades; and we are unable to think practically about the tasks that relate to it. The danger of surrounding the temple of war with this too-sacred boundary is that the fascination it evokes cuts us off from practical responsibility.

It is better for practical reason, perhaps, not to try to be too clear about precisely where 'peace' ends and 'war' begins, or to mark where moral rules 'towards' war end and moral rules 'in' war take over. For the principles of judgment that divide responsible action from irresponsible, charitable action from uncharitable, disciplined from undisciplined, are very much the same.

This invites a concluding remark about what I may call the 'spirituality' of the armed-judgment proposal. It conceives itself as a discipline of deliberation, a way of focussing and posing questions of political responsibility to oneself and to others at that frontier of human experience where action is in danger of breaking down into mere reaction. It is an expression of faith – perhaps in the teeth of primary experience – in the providential gift of honest judgment as a praxis in which the whole political community can be involved. Its purpose is to keep the scope for judgment *open*, the different points at which judgment is exercised *distinct*; to avoid wrapping everything up globally and precipitately.

One doctrine of the classic just war thinkers very much disparaged in modern debate is that the common soldier could and should presume the justice of his prince's decisions until persuaded otherwise. This has elicited predictable complaints about its undemocratic presuppositions and its underestimate of the common soldier's judgment; but these betray a misunderstanding. Its point was precisely to allow *more* scope for the soldier to exercise judgment *about his own actions*. It denied, in other words, that the only decisions worth considering were the decisions of the prince. If the ordinary soldier had first to reach a clear and informed view of the right and wrong of the prince's decision – the question which of all questions he was least equipped to answer, simply from the point of view of access to the relevant information – he could never get to the point of considering his own rôle and responsibility. It was, of course, acknowledged that the point could be reached where a private soldier understood the cause he supported as insupportable; and at that point he must extricate himself from it as best he could. But the point of the proposal was not to try to resolve that point first, working theoretically and deductively downwards from a premiss, 'this war is just', to a permissive conclusion, 'I may take part in it'. It was to mount a deliberative exploration outwards from a given point of practical engagement: what does the praxis of judgment require of *me*, a soldier, in *this* armed conflict *now*? – an exploration which may *possibly* lead to the discovery that the praxis of judgment has been compromised too greatly by superiors and comrades to allow continued co-operation, but will have a great deal of more immediate concern to sort out first.

Loss of this deliberative perspective in the modern world has helped to empty the citizen's responsibilities of practical significance, reducing us all to the status of amateur journalists and commentators. 'Are you in favour of, or against, United States policy?' That is the only form, apparently, in which a moral question about war can ever be put, even to those of us who are supposedly citizens of other countries which have their own policies. As soon as the first hint of future conflict passes across the airwaves, we are all on hand with our own editorials, condemning or supporting the hostilities before a shot has been fired, castigating the United States or being loyal to it, vigorously promoting that polarisation of public opinion which in our wiser moments we deplore. The opinionated public constitutes a positive obstacle to deliberation about the praxis of judgment. It does the opposite of what citizens of a state at war ought to do, which is to deliberate *with* their government and army, so providing a sounding-board for the serious exercise of judgment on alternative courses of action. A deliberating public would move forward with its military and political representatives from situation to situation, treating each next decision as different from the last one, listening to reasons with an open mind and asking demanding questions about the explanations offered, bearing in mind that there is much it cannot know, but also that there is much *they* cannot know either. A deliberating public would keep the scope for judgment open at each step, not foreclosing future history with a stonking battery of Yes or No let fire on Day Minus One. A deliberating public would elicit a more conscientious performance from its representatives, political and military. And a deliberating public would observe much more sharply if the point were reached at which those representatives stepped outside the praxis of judgment and reverted to the lawless extravagances of antagonistic confrontation. The worst crimes in war tend to be committed later in its course, when patience and discipline have worn thin. But by the time the leaders of the nations are driven to resort to the worst excesses of wickedness, the public has so exhausted its rhetorical resources that it is liable to let the fact pass without notice.

2 Authority

The classic just-war thinkers, as we have said, traced a moral analogy between ordinary acts of judgment internal to government and a praxis of judgment that used the means of armed conflict to reach beyond the self-contained and self-complacent sphere of the autonomous political society to deal with crimes committed by nations against each other. The conception is expressed by Suárez: 'The only reason for it' – i.e., that the same person acts paradoxically both as plaintiff and judge – 'is that an act of punitive justice was indispensable to mankind, and that no more fitting means for it was forthcoming within the limits of nature and human action.'[16] What distinguishes the justified resort to armed conflict is the unavailability of ordinary means of judgment. Justice in war stood in relation to the exercise of domestic justice as an emergency operation, performed in a remote mountain-hut with a penknife, stands to the same surgery performed under clinical conditions in a hospital. The reason for carrying the practice outside the ordinary institutions of government is simply the emergency: it was 'indispensible to mankind'. But the grossness of the means excludes their use in less pressing circumstances. Judgment

[16] Francisco Suárez, *De triplici virtute theologica* 3.13.4.7 (*IG*, p. 739).

in armed conflict is extraordinary, an adventure beyond the ordinary reach of law and order, hazarded upon God's providential provision. 'It may be that YHWH will act for us; nothing can hinder YHWH from saving by many or by few.'[17]

Yet Suárez, like other classic just-war thinkers, cherished the hope that if the implicitly principled character of this emergency operation were brought to light, the principles on which it was conducted would be seen as normative *without* the constant need for resort to extraordinary means. It is as though the operation improvised in the mountain-hut were a catalyst for the foundation of a network of cottage hospitals in remote areas, capable of providing immediate emergency care on a regular basis. The beckoning prospect of an international law lured these thinkers on to what may sometimes appear a too relentless exploration of what were, after all, supposed to be exceptional measures. Some theologians of more recent times, while admitting the possibility of justifiable armed conflict, have been reluctant to discuss the conditions for it, lest such discussion serve to normalise the extraordinary.[18] The classic just-war thinkers, on the other hand, hoped that by exploring the logic of the extraordinary case exhaustively, they could bring to light the underlying ordinariness of the principle so as to make it more effective in ordinary practice. Judgment in war was extraordinary in that it arose out of the failure of all ordinary means, but ordinary in that it was governed by the same principles as the ordinary means. So it held out the promise of extending the ordinary means and widening the scope of ordinary judgment to encompass international disputes.

What are the extraordinary features? They are two: first, that armed conflict typically extends a government's power beyond the

---

[17] 1 Sam. 14:6. Cf. Ps. 20:7: 'Some trust in chariots, some in horses . . . we trust in YHWH.' The Psalmist is certainly not *refusing* chariots and horses, but claims a different ground of confidence from that of military powers and warrior cultures.

[18] So I understand Karl Barth. See my 'Karl Barth and Ramsey's "Uses of Power"', in Oliver O'Donovan and Joan Lockwood O'Donovan, *Bonds of Imperfection*, Grand Repids, Eerdmans, 2003.

limits of its sphere of authority; secondly, it typically deploys force without a judicial inquisition. The belligerent power attempts to impose decisions on a community not lawfully subject to it, and the forces it intends to destroy receive no formal trial and are found guilty of no charge. The fact that we can identify these two differences, and not just one, warns us that the typical exercise of government and the typical praxis of international warfare do not between them exhaust all possibilities. There are two intermediate variant types. Civil war, waged against a rebellion, is one of them. Here a government imposes decisions upon its own subject communities, but not by ordinary judicial means. The other variant, where judicial process is used but outside the government's sphere of authority, is more exotic. The trial and execution in Jerusalem of Adolf Eichmann, the German war criminal whose crimes were committed on German soil against German citizens before the very foundation of the state which made him answerable to justice, affords one striking and exceptional instance. Had either German state chosen to take serious exception to Israel's unilateral assertion of judicial responsibility, it would have given rise to a most bizarre form of international conflict. However, some rather similar issues were raised more recently between Spain and Chile in the Pinochet case. The UN Convention on Torture, which imposes a duty on states to try cases not arising within their jurisdiction, suggests that this other variant may be less uncommon in future than it has been hitherto.

It may seem that to identify these two extraordinary features of war is to ignore a third and more obvious one: that war does damage on a much greater scale than ordinary acts of judgment. Obvious as this may seem to us, who are used to modern conditions in which government is not usually sanguinary and war is excessively so, we must remember that these conditions are not universal. Within adult memory we have seen governments behaving in so dreadfully sanguinary a fashion that recourse has been had to war simply to put a halt to the bloodshed. We have also seen bloodless military coups that killed nobody. It is not essential to warmaking that you should kill, merely that you should intend to remove by all necessary means the forces that oppose you. The scale of loss of life, important as it is in any concrete moral decision, does not define the distinctive nature of war as such.

It may seem, alternatively, that these two extraordinary features can be reduced to one. When a government has to proceed against its own subjects without judicial process, we could argue, it has clearly lost authority. Civil war is a measure to which governments resort only when they can no longer call on the ordinary procedures of judicial control. It appears, then, that it is merely a special case of the general rule that war is a venture of power beyond the scope of civil authority. But even if we concede this connexion between them, we must still note that there are two quite distinct ways in which a belligerent party may lack authority: (a) because the cause lies *outside* its sphere of authority from the start; (b) because its authority *within* its sphere has collapsed. When British and American bombers imposed upon Iraq the judicial rulings of the Security Council that limited Iraq's freedom of flight over its Kurdish and Arab regions, that raised one difficulty: British and American forces had no civil authority over Iraq's territiory. When the British SAS gunned down terrorists in the streets of Gibraltar, that raised another difficulty: though British forces had civil authority in Gibraltar, there was no judicial process prior to execution. These two difficulties remain quite different, even if they are each in different ways generated by problems in the exercise of authority.

We begin, then, with some questions about the first of the two extraordinary factors, and ask whether and how an act that reaches outside the scope of an agent's authority may, nevertheless, be authorised. An act of judgment must have authority, for it must be a public act, not a private act of vengeance. Only public acts may legitimately call upon the use of force. Only governments may make war, for the same reason that only police and magistrates may arrest and only judges sentence, namely, that they require representative persons, acting for the community, to perform them. Yet with no public authority in the international realm, how can there be such a thing as a 'public act' in war? It has seemed to many thinkers that an international realm made up of sovereign states is simply not susceptible of any claim to public authority. 'No war of independent states against each other can be a *punitive* war (*bellum punitivum*),' Kant wrote. 'For punishment occurs only in the relation of a superior (*imperantis*) to those subject to him (*subditum*), and states do not stand in that relation to each other.'[19] This argument rules out not only the penal cause of war as strictly understood, but the whole conception of war as an authorised act of judgment. The antagonistic form of the act of war, Kant implies, excludes the presence of authority. And so it has appeared that the only way to conceive of justified war is to treat all war as 'private war', i.e., true *duellum*, and to justify it simply as a pre-political act of self-defence against aggression. From this arises the modern tendency to reduce the causes of war to the single cause of national self-defence.

The classic just-war thinkers could not think of it in that way, for they thought that the antagonistic structure of self-defence was itself morally problematic for Christians. There was an evangelical duty (or, from another theological position, an evangelical counsel) of non-resistance to evil. They hoped to show, on the contrary, that behind the antagonistic appearance of the typical war might lie an implicit structure of authorised arbitration. Francisco di Vitoria gave eloquent expression to this thought in the conclusion of his famous lecture on the law of war: 'The victor must think of himself as a judge sitting in judgment between two commonwealths, one the injured party and the other the offender; he must not pass sentence as the prosecutor, but as a judge. He must give satisfaction to the injured, but as far as possible without causing the utter ruination of the guilty

---

[19] Immanuel Kant, *The Metaphysics of Morals*, the Doctrine of Right, 57. Trans. Mary Gregor, Cambridge, Cambridge University Press, 1991, p. 153.

commonwealth.'[20] The judicial posture demanded in that passage of the victor was demanded, too, of the belligerent, not yet a victor, but hoping to be. Even the pursuit of war must be in a judicial spirit, acting as though one is not merely defending one's own interests but deciding an issue between claimants.

By definition war arises in the absence of an adequate formal authority to resolve a dispute. But public order abhors a vacuum. The just belligerent is supposed to venture, informally and with extraordinary means, the judgment that *would* be made by a formal court, *if* there were a competent one. This move clearly identifies the proposal with a natural law rather than a positive law orientation. Institutions of right are called forth by the relations of right themselves; they are not foundational for the relations of right. Anyone can see, of course, that such an conception offers scope for moral self-deception. But if the belligerent deceives himself, he deceives himself *about something*. He deceives himself in thinking that his act of war is justifiable *in principle*, i.e., that an ideal judge would act as he is acting, or would authorise his conduct. To be deceived in such a thought, the thought must be intelligible. That is to say, the idea of an ideal judgment which would or would not authorise this act of war must be a coherent moral idea. If the hypothesis of the ideal judge is unthinkable, the self-deception is impossible.

The outline of such an ideal judgment is in fact always present in the world in the form of public sentiment, quick to approve or disapprove what is done on the international stage. Even with no judge to pronounce, public sentiment can, and will, pronounce. So public sentiment sows the dragon's teeth from which an authorised army springs to life. But public sentiment is not purely arbitrary; it appeals, like the belligerents themselves, to *right*. The question of the right of a case will always engage us on its own terms, independently of the question whether and how anyone, even public sentiment,

---

[20] Francisco di Vitoria, *De iure belli relectio* 3.9.60, in *Vitoria: Political Writings*, ed. Anthony Pagden and Jeremy Lawrance, Cambridge, Cambridge University Press, 1991, p. 327.

has authority to *decide* the right. We cannot make our thought about justice stand still in its tracks, and confine itself to the dicta of publicly recognised authorities. The same train of moral reflection which can point to what a competent judicial authority 'would' allow, or 'would' do, can also point to what a competent public sentiment 'would' approve of, if it were fully informed and dispassionate. Such trains of thought are, of course, indefinitely open to contest; and that is why where formally constituted authorities exist, it is they, not the ideal ones, that must be obeyed. But where they do not exist, or do not operate effectively, we cannot silence the question of whether an international act of war or abstention from war *is after all* just; and by the same token we cannot refuse the possibility of informal pronouncements which carry moral authority. This moral necessity provides the point of reference for talk of an 'implicitly judicial' structure of acts of war.

Nowadays any power contemplating a resort to war has more than a hypothetical or informal judgment to think about. Just as in the Middle Ages there was a Pope and a Holy Roman Emperor, whose authorisation in these matters counted for something, so today there is the United Nations Organisation and its Security Council. To the judgment of this body there belongs not merely moral but positive authority, grounded originally in treaty. Its Charter claims for it the sole right to authorise or use armed force against states other than that undertaken for self-defence against armed attack.[21] A belligerent power, then, ought to be prepared to defer to it, even if it sometimes rules in a way that a truly impartial and well-informed judge would not have ruled, for courts have authority even when they are mistaken in particulars. However, courts, too, may lose authority altogether, whether by constant malfunction or by inability to enact their judgments; and the UNO, often paralysed by superpower stand-offs, regional politics or the unwillingness of members

---

[21] Charter of the United Nations art. 39–51, in Ian Brownlie, ed., *Basic Documents in International Law*, Oxford, Oxford University Press, 5th edn, 2002, pp. 11–13.

to support its decisions, has a very patchy record for getting a firm grip on conflicts. Its achievement in the Gulf crisis of 1991 and its unsatisfactory involvements in subsequent crises in Somalia and ex-Yugoslavia constitute a hopeful indication of a rôle it may yet play, not a decisive proof that it can play it. So we are not in the position where we could say there is no longer any room for informal authority to act without formal authorisation. Nor will we ever be in that position, since there can be no guarantee that even a very strong UNO would not develop serious failures in its practice and lose authority. What we are in a position to say, however, is that a much *greater* burden of proof now rests on any party that would take forcible action unilaterally, and that the aim of international policy must be to strengthen the UNO's authority, and so make the burden of proof greater still.

So we have identified two conditions for the authority to venture judgment in war: (a) the existence of a conspicuous right, and (b) the want of a formal institution to enforce it. Under those circumstances a government may, and sometimes must, step outside its ordinary sphere of authority into the rôle of a third party, institutionally vacant but morally required by the general public reflection, in order to maintain the right in international conflict. It acts judicially in arbitrating the claims of the two parties to the conflict. The fact that moral authority to make war is at root a judicial authority allows two inferences. (i) Acts of war carry with them the responsibility to care for the right of both parties equally. A belligerent has to act for 'the' right, not 'our' right. (ii) The authority to exercise judgment over a hostile power is limited to the settling of the cause which has occasioned the conflict, and does not imply the assumption of all the rights and duties of a ruler. Any given exercise of judgment is determinate, concerned with a particular cause and not with all causes; and this extraordinary exercise, because it is extraordinary, is limited to the point at issue. Victory, in other words, is not a title of conquest. The classic just-war thinkers allowed the victor a fairly generous material compensation, which may often have had the effect of transferring whole communities from one jurisdiction to another; but their permissions were couched in terms of property, not jurisdiction.

In order to mark this restriction more sharply, John Locke propounded what he called the 'strange doctrine' that 'the power a conqueror gets over those he overcomes in a just war is perfectly despotical; he has an absolute power over the lives of those who, by putting themselves in a state of war, have forfeited them, but he has not thereby a right and title to their possessions'.[22] What makes the doctrine strange, however, is only the author's characteristic reverence for landholding as the essence of a people's tradition: 'the father by his miscarriages and violence can forfeit but his own life . . . His goods which Nature . . . hath made to belong to the children to keep them from perishing, do still continue to belong to his children.' Freed of landholding mysticism, the truth can be put more simply, and even appear commonplace: the right to govern depends not solely upon force and the exercise of judgment, but upon the tradition of the governed. Intervention into the affairs of another people, however necessary and justified in itself, constitutes no authority to rule them.

To this general statement, however, we shall have to make two important qualifications. To see why, we must explore two common moral intuitions which run somewhat counter to the account we have given so far. First, we are instinctively more hesitant to license wars of intervention in defence of third parties than we are to license wars of national self-defence. Yet on the judicial model the war of intervention presents a rather better case of war as arbitration, and ought to be easier to justify. Secondly, we instinctively find armed revolution more difficult to justify than war against external powers. Yet on the judicial model revolution should be justifiable on precisely the same terms as foreign war, namely that as a government's authority erodes,

---

[22] John Locke, *Second Treatise of Government*, 180–2. Ed. P. Laslett, Cambridge, Cambridge University Press, 2nd edn, 1988, pp. 388–9.

there is a judicial vacuum that may be filled informally by any party acting in defence of conspicuous right.

How seriously should we take these contrary intuitions? We might argue that they are irrelevant: the proposal is, after all, a radically evangelical proposal for reinterpreting armed conflict in terms of judgment, and so takes issue from the outset with the generally antagonistic shape of our natural intuitions about war. These specific intuitions may be no more than hangovers from the unregenerate idea of war as unmediated opposition; they both display a statist tendency, valuing the preservation of existing political order above justice itself, and this tendency may betray an unevangelical origin and character. Yet it is not necessary to take such a high-handed way with them. There is a legitimate concern that lurks behind their apparently statist sentiments: the formal authority of political structures, on which the task of judgment depends, must not simply be swept away by an enthusiasm to improvise judgment whenever and however it appears to be needed. Judgment has need of its settled institutions, too, and we must mind that they are properly respected. The evangelical proposal needs to keep faith with that limited endorsement which St Paul accords in Romans 13 to 'the authorities that exist'.

To complete our account, therefore, we need to add a third condition for the authority to exercise judgment in armed conflict, (c): an existing representative status, which authorises a belligerent party to judge the causes of its own people. The classic just-war thinkers used to say that an aggressor, by injuring another people, put itself under the jurisdiction of that people's prince. As it stands, this is a puzzling assertion; but it can be made comprehensible with some reformulation. The government of the injured people extends the sphere of its existing authority into an institutional vacuum. It projects, as it were, its general responsibility for the causes of its people into a situation where the opposing party is a foreign people. One party lies outside its normal sphere of jurisdiction, but the other lies fully within it. This conception will, I believe, break the stranglehold of the notion that war is essentially duellistic, based on the right of national self-defence. The connexion between the authority to make war and the status of injured party is given by the *existing responsibility* which the government bears for its people. In grasping this, we can understand how even acts of war have been interpreted within the tradition as extraordinary acts of love, providing, in the first place, the judgment of which the injured neighbour stands in need, but not excluding love for the injured neighbour's enemy at the same time.

International doctrine since 1945 has witnessed a growing disagreement as to whether it is too limiting to restrict authority to the government of an injured people. Can there be a justified act of intervention, especially for the purpose of some kind of international rescue? In the debates surrounding the controversial NATO bombing of Kosovo in 1999 the precedents most commonly cited were the intervention of India in East Pakistan in 1972, which opened the way to the creation of the state of Bangladesh, the intervention of Tanzania in Uganda in 1977 to rescue it from a sanguinary tyranny, and the more recent intervention of West African states to restore order in Liberia and Sierra Leone. There is little difficulty with the idea of intervention when it is invited by a government itself authorised to act. That brings it within the category of a defensive alliance; and alliances have an important role in stabilising international affairs by providing a guarantee of effective action which will warn off potential aggressors. The difficulties arise where the invitation is not given, or, if given, is of questionable legality. May one party to a civil war invite an outsider to assist them? Or may a people without nation-statehood and lacking the legal competence to form a defensive alliance, like the Kurds in Iraq, invite a sovereign power to defend them against their government?

The legal position in contemporary international law remains disputed. We should observe, however, that international law, like all law, needs to be developed in relation to cases; but lacking the courts to develop it, it can too easily become locked into an abstractly doctrinaire posture. Its authority can only be damaged if it is held to prohibit actions which people in general are inclined to think not only justifiable, but even morally obligatory. There may well be dangers attached to the kind of humanitarian intervention which has been argued for; but they need to be overwhelmingly conspicuous if they are to provide support for a universal prohibition running counter to the humanitarian instincts of civilised peoples. To turn one's back while a neighbouring community is being slaughtered is not an easy thing to recommend; and international law should not demand it without reasons so strong as to seem, when pointed out, morally irresistible. Certainly, the maintenance of a 'rather tidy legal regime' based on the sovereignty of the nation-state will not suffice.[23] Yet it is appropriate to expect that any such intervention will be carried out by parties with a demonstrable interest in the welfare of those they propose to rescue – not *self*-interest, of course, which is, at best, irrelevant, but that altruistic interest which comes from being kin, or neighbours, or from long cultural ties. 'Regional interests' are not to be despised as a ground for moral authorisation. A power that intervenes has to be a credible representative. In the Gulf War of 1991 it was an essential element of the alliance's justification that the Gulf states were active in promoting it out of Arab solidarity and neighbourly concern.

The same principle, that we look for some representative status on the part of those who resort to war on others' behalf, sheds light on the historically much discussed question of *justified rebellion*. In the crisis of the Protestant Reformation, as the German princes found themselves threatened by the military might of Emperor Charles V, the idea became current that there could be a constitutional act of resistance on the part of lawful regional authorities to a lawful central government. This thought, first floated by Philip of Hesse, was novel in breaking with the late-medieval corporatist assumption that a monarch was restrained by nobles *acting together*, as the Pope

---

[23] A pleasingly self-mocking phrase from Ian Brownlie, *International Law and the Use of Force by States Revisited*, Oxford, Europaeum, 2000, p. 12, which argues the case against a right of humanitarian intervention in international law.

was restrained by the Bishops in a General Council. This essentially parliamentary concept is still to the fore in the discussion of a class of 'ephors' which takes its rise from Calvin and comes to its fullest expression in Johannes Althusius, which therefore makes little substantial advance upon the concepts of constitutional representation current in the fifteenth century. Philip, on the other hand, asserted the right of German princes to act *independently*, possibly drawing on an ancient feudal concept that barons never spoke as a council, but only individually, each for his own vassalage. Thus was proposed the defence of a *part* of the realm which aimed, not at the restraint or deposition of the monarch, but at secession, whether temporary or permanent, from the political society which the monarch's rule defined. It summoned those who enjoyed representative status within the oppressed part of the society to assume full responsibility and so, in effect, found a new political society.

This point sharpens the distinction between responsible rebellion, as it was classically envisaged by emerging nations at the dawn of the nation-state era, and what is experienced today under the name of 'terrorism'. Terrorism names a historical conjunction of two distinct phenomena: the waging of war by disordered means, in defiance of proportion or (especially) discrimination, and the waging of war by military organisations which are not only *not* governments, or subject to governments, but are not even *putative* governments, and so have no direct interest in the provision of judgment for any community which they plunge into the turmoil of armed struggle. This attitude was classically exemplified by the curious self-consciousness of the Irish Republican Army, which thought itself constitutionally incompetent to make any political decision for the public good. Basing itself on a curious contractarian-nationalist belief that no government in Ireland could be legitimate unless chosen by a single act of the whole Irish people – it was not widely understood outside Ireland that doctrinaire republicans denied the legitimacy of the Republic of Ireland – it conceived that in the absence of a legitimate government, Ireland could be represented only by an army, floating free and politically unaccountable, devoted to military but not to political ends. Such a liberation of force from political constraints was at once a reversion to a primitive heroic culture and the fruit of a quasi-Marxist philosophy that social and political forms evolved by historical necessity, so that resistance could be its own end, with no goal in view other than making civil order break down, so nudging historical necessity, as it were, along its foreordained path.

This strategy of *ressentiment*, in which the taste for denial gets the upper hand of the thirst for power, differs totally from that of rebellion; for an act of ordered rebellion is itself the first step out of the mentality of denial, positing a new political order which agents of rebellion accept the responsibility for bringing about. To say this much, of course, is not to issue a general licence to rebellion; it is simply to establish the ground on which rebellion, but not terrorism, might possibly lay claim to *authority*. The questions of material justice in the cause and conduct of an armed conflict, which a rebellion, like any other act of war, must satisfy, would remain to be settled in any given case.

We need, then, to qualify in a second way our earlier separation of the authority to exercise judgment from the authority to rule. We have already said that only those who ruled one interested party, or plausibly represented them, might assert the right to judge the other. Now we must add that even though there can be no right of conquest to rule the other party, there must be a responsibility to ensure that the other party is ruled. Nobody could undertake to depose the Taliban, in however worthy a cause, without taking serious steps to enable the emergence of a representative government for Afghanistan. To disavow the tasks of 'nation-building' is simply to renounce the conditions of doing justice. War is always unjustified if it is antagonistic; and it is essentially antagonistic if it does not intend the state of peaceful and lawful governance for the community against which war is waged. An act of judgment is a lawgiving act; it provides for the good order of future relations within a community and among communities. So an act of judgment would be incomplete if it left either party to the conflict without government by law, which is the will of God for both.

Terrorism forces us, as nothing else does, to recognise the indispensability of government. If it is one aspect of the just-war proposal to rein in the excessive claims of state sovereignty by subjecting every government to the terms of international justice, another aspect is to stress the unique rôle of governments as the agents of international justice. Non-governmental organisations, whether military or social, can never claim the representative status that entitles a government to judge; and without judgment a state of ordered peace among and within the nations cannot command the authority of law. It is the essential structure of government to harness representative status and power to the service of judgment and law. That structure is the provision of common grace, and without it our best efforts at making peace are doomed to be swept away.

3 Discrimination

At the heart of the project of subjecting armed conflict to the disciplines of judgment stands what has been called in modern times the 'principle of discrimination'. Separating the innocent from the guilty is the object of judgment, the intention that defines it. To pursue this object by armed conflict is to make a decisive break with the antagonistic conception, for which what counts is 'our' self-defence against 'their' hostility. It forces us to see that 'we' and 'they' in any conflict are not absolute terms, but are open to further analysis. The collectivity of a people is not a herd or mass, but a politically representative structure in which one acts for others. 'It does not suffice that we conceive the enemy, by some fiction, as though they were a single body,' Grotius remarks, speaking for the whole of the classic just-war tradition.[24] To be discriminate is to enquire into who acts

---

[24] Hugo Grotius, *De iure belli ac pacis* 3.11.16.2., ed. B.J.A. de Kanter-van Hettinga Tromp, R. Feenstra and C.E. Persenaire, Aalen, Germany, Scientia Verlag, 1993, p. 759.

for whom, and how. That enquiry is the greatest moral safeguard we have against totalitarian claims to loyalty made on behalf of the nation-state or of any other popular formation.

In the early and middle part of the twentieth century the notions of discriminate attack, non-combatant immunity, legitimate targets and so on, which in the past couple of decades have dominated Western ideas of the just conduct of war, were virtually unknown to the intelligent public. In the literature on the ethics of war which both the First and the Second World War produced it hardly appears. So C.S. Lewis responded sceptically to a prayer of penitence offered in church after the bombing of Hiroshima in 1945, writing in a letter: 'If what we have since heard is true, i.e. that the first item on the Japanese anti-invasion programme was the killing of every European in Japan, the answer did not to me seem so simple as all that.'[25] Although the principle of discrimination had shaped the Conventions of the Hague (1899, 1907), it had quickly been eroded, principally as a result of the invention of the aeroplane. As the Hague regulations pre-dated air combat, a legal vacuum opened up around the use of the aeroplane in war. The argument for 'strategic air war', i.e., bombing raids upon centres of population, became a standard part of the infant air-forces' campaign for equal recognition as an armed service. Strategic air war, though it proved inconclusive in the Second World War, survived to become the centre-piece of post-war deterrence stategy.[26] Given the events of August 1945, it was not surprising that when the Geneva Conventions of 1949 attempted to update and consolidate the legacy of laws of war in the light of recent experience, the vacuum in this area was left unaddressed.

Three factors, however, contributed to a recovery of the principle of discrimination in international law and in public consciousness.

[25] C.S. Lewis, *Letters*, ed. W.H. Lewis, London, Geoffrey Bles, 1966, p. 225.

[26] Cf. my *Peace and Certainty: A Theological Essay on Deterrence*, Oxford, Oxford University Press & Grand Rapids, Eerdmans, 1989, pp. 31–53, for some reflections on the intellectual history of the deterrence idea. Lawrence Freedman, *The Evolution of Nuclear Strategy*, London, Macmillan, 1981 provides a thorough institutional history.

First there was the work of the International Committee of the Red Cross, charged to repair omissions from the Geneva Conventions; this resulted in the Two Geneva Protocols of 1977, in the first of which an obligation was laid upon all belligerents to 'distinguish between the civilian population and combatants … and direct their operations only against military objectives'.[27] Secondly there was the massive public disquiet over nuclear weapons, in the debate over which the just-war condemnation of indiscriminate attack was widely appealed to. In this debate Christians played a decisive rôle; for the revival of interest in classic just-war categories, fuelled precisely by their relevance to strategic warfare, had begun in Roman Catholic circles in the 1920s, and by the 1960s was becoming common coin among Western Christians. It had a notable last-minute influence upon the Second Vatican Council, where a late revision to the text of *Gaudium et Spes* condemned in very solemn terms 'the indiscriminate destruction of whole cities or vast areas with their inhabitants'.[28]

The third factor was the modifications which NATO doctrines of deterrence underwent in the 1960s, yielding the so-called 'doctrine of flexible response'. These modifications were prompted by the recognition that counter-city postures of massive deterrence were hopelessly inflexible in a crisis. The need to find lower levels of nuclear response created a significant reversal in the direction of weapon technology, away from enhanced power towards precision-targeting. This new technology, conceived at first for nuclear use, was then adapted to conventional warfare, and its effects were seen on a large scale for the first time in the Gulf War of 1991, which also provided the first test of the 1977 Protocols (observed in practice by the alliance,

[27] I Gen. Prot. 48. In Adam Roberts and Richard Guelff, eds, *Documents on the Laws of War*, 2nd edn, Oxford, Oxford University Press, 1989, p. 414.

[28] *Gaudium et Spes* 80, in A. Flannery, OP, ed., *Vatican Council II: the Conciliar and Post Conciliar Documents*, 1988, vol. I, pp. 989–90. For the background debate, cf. Paul Ramsey, *The Just War*, New York, Scribners, 1969, pp. 369–90. A certain impact of Christian concerns on superpower policy, though it was never extensive, may be seen in the success of the US Catholic Bishops in eliciting from the US Government in 1983 a satisfactory clarification about the nuclear targeting of Soviet installations.

though not legally binding, since they were not adhered to by both parties). In the second half of the twentieth century, then, the notion of discrimination came to seem more significant as the destructive possibilities of strategic warfare became more evident.

Discrimination is, however, not an easy idea to define, and it offers more than a little scope for talking at cross-purposes. The First Geneva Protocol characterises an 'indiscriminate attack' in three ways: (i) it is 'not directed at a specific military target'; (ii) it employs a 'method or means of combat which cannot be directed at a military objective'; (iii) it employs 'a method or means of combat the effects of which cannot be limited'. Indiscriminate attacks, it concludes, are 'of a nature to strike military objectives and civilians or civilian objects without distinction'.[29] Of these three characterisations the second seems to define an empty class. The third is strictly a definition of a type of disproportion. What is needed in a definition of discrimination is a focus on the *intention of the attack*, as in the first limb. In widening the definition to include methods and means, there must be a link back to the intention by way of what it would be reasonable to expect to happen. Thus the Inhumane Weapons Convention of 1981, repeating the triple characterisation, correctly rewrites the third limb to say that indiscriminate use '*may be expected* to cause incidental loss of civilian life, injury to civilians, damage to civilian objects . . . which would be excessive in relation to the concrete and direct military advantage anticipated'.[30] If excessive damage may be expected, it may be assumed intended; if intended, then indiscriminate. We shall return to the logic of this presumption in a moment. Popular use of the term 'indiscriminate' is, of course, much looser, and sometimes seems to mean no more than 'badly aimed' or 'inaccurate'.

We shall define a discriminate act of conflict as one that *intends to make a distinction between guilt and innocence*. We need to explore

---

[29] I Gen. Prot. 51.4. (Roberts and Guelff, eds, *Documents*, pp. 415–16).
[30] Inhumane Weapons Convention, prot. 2.3 (ibid., p. 480).

two aspects of this: the sense in which *guilt and innocence* is relevant to acts of armed conflict, and the nature of the *intention to distinguish* between the two.

Guilt and innocence

Someone engaged in armed conflict intends a distinction between guilt and innocence when he acts to overcome *direct material co-operation in the doing of wrong*. Here no mention need be made of the distinction between military and civilian targets, nor even of the more nuanced distinction between combatant and non-combatant personnel. Much of the time these amount to the same thing, but not always. The expression 'material co-operation in the doing of wrong' reveals the morally relevant factor that allows us to treat enemy combatants as putatively guilty – namely, their practical engagement in an act that will wrong others.

The notion of guilt applicable to combatants in war is not the same as that applicable to a criminal gang. The latter is a voluntary association of individuals who have conspired to commit a crime; the former are the designated military representatives of their political community, connected to it by innocent bonds of birth or by civil membership. So the concept of guilt can only be extended to soldiers by analogy. Yet the analogy, which turns on the notion of material co-operation, is a necessary one. Combatant soldiers are not guilty of their people's aggression in the same sense that even the weakest-minded members of a criminal enterprise are guilty; yet since they co-operate directly in the perpetration of wrong, they incur a decisive liability in the course of their execution of it.

The phenomenon of corporate responsibility cannot be assimilated entirely to personal guilt, on the one hand, or to helpless, and so innocent, involvement on the other. It implies a morally substantive relation to the community that has blundered into culpable ways, incurring liabilities short of outright personal punishment. Grotius describes it as 'median guilt', *culpa media*, which 'is liable for restitution, but usually not for punishment'.[31] The idea of corporate responsibility does not imply that everybody is equally culpable or is culpable in the same manner; there are different ways of being implicated in a common guilt incurred by the society as a whole. The civilian at home and the soldier in the field may each be personally innocent of the crime of fomenting war; yet each incurs a liability, the civilian to material loss, and the combatant to direct attack. This latter liability arises quite particularly and exclusively while he is *actively engaged* in hostilities. At that point he counts as guilty, because at that point he is the immediate agent, willing or unwilling, of the culpable assault. But when he surrenders, he becomes inviolable, subject to no further restraint than is necessary to prevent his bearing arms again.

This inviolability is, according to Grotius, a truth of the Natural Law, a delivery of rational morality. 'There is no danger from prisoners and from those who have surrendered or desire to do so.'[32] Involvement in collective guilt does not make us liable to penal execution for an offence of which we are not subjectively guilty. It exposes us only to attack while we positively co-operate in the collective wrongdoing. But it is one of those startling discrepancies which, in Grotius's view, arise between Natural Law and the Law of Nations that the latter, basing itself on the classical theory that a surrendered soldier's life was at the disposal of his captor, permitted him to be enslaved. This tradition he can defend only by treating it as an immunity granted as an incentive to desist from slaughter. Here, he thought, was a case where the positive law adopted a merely restraining rôle in curbing human impulses to evil. For the duty to spare the surrendered was, he thought, a universal moral obligation. We have suggested that it is more properly thought of as an evangelical one.[33]

---

[31] Grotius, *De iure* 3.11.4.8, p. 746.   [32] Ibid., 3.11.16.1, p. 758.

[33] Either way, the widespread shudder of dismay when the American Defence Secretary seemed to suggest that surrendered foreign fighters in Afghanistan might be summarily executed was hardly a surprising or exaggerated response, given the tradition of civilised practice in Christendom.

The modern practice of conscription does not as such affect the logic of combatant responsibility. Indeed, it makes it clearer, by emphasising that armed forces act *only* as their society's representatives. It has never been true, I think, that wars were fought entirely at the behest of armies, but career armies could make that construction seem plausible. Civilian populations, capable of infinite self-deceit, are not unwilling to be told that wars are caused by soldiers, arms manufacturers, international capitalists, or whatever, when in truth they are caused by civil societies with ambitions, good or bad in themselves, that carry a price-tag in international conflict. Conscription has the socially desirable result that societies must study the price-tag on their policies. Yet there are major disadvantages, too: most obviously, it exposes the young (and traditionally, the young males) to the greatest danger. Conscript armies, moreover, are not generally well trained and cannot be relied upon to maintain high standards of conduct.

Material co-operation in wrong is not confined to armed forces. The politicians who dictate the policy, the information technologists who handle communications, the mechanics who service the hardware, the administrative staff on whom the logistics depend, all these co-operate directly and materially in wrongdoing. A well-aimed missile might knock out a mechanic, a politician, a computer operator and a driver, all technically 'civilians', without causing one truly non-combatant death. On the other hand a doctor, a chef, a lawyer and a plumber may all be in uniform, and yet effectively non-combatants. Drawing the line can be a nice matter: provisioning an army on campaign is an obviously an act of material co-operation, while selling food to the army or preparing it for consumption is doing no more than would be done in peacetime. Yet while we puzzle over the twilight cases, we cannot overlook the difference between day and night: a soldier in his tank is a combatant, his wife and children in an air-raid shelter are non-combatants.

What are we to say of the 'innocence' of the non-combatant? It is as different from the criminal conception of innocence as is the guilt of the combatant from the criminal conception of guilt; yet the analogy, again, is a necessary one. It is not put in question by the moral support that non-combatants afford to their state's war effort, perhaps by working overtime in their civilian rôles to make up for those engaged in military duties. The innocence in question is simply that of not being materially co-operative with wrongful hostilities. There are, no doubt, many kinds of guilt by complicity that are plausibly attributed to non-combatant populations of belligerent states. But it is not *that kind* of guilt which the act of judgment deals with, but merely the guilt of direct material co-operation. Those columns of unarmed Muslim refugees, which from time to time were used by Bosnian Serb forces as targets for shooting-practice, were, without doubt, great sympathisers with the Bosnian government cause, even before they were driven from their homes and shot at. But that did not make them combatants.

The notion of guilt by combatancy corresponds roughly, but not exactly, to the common contention that in making war we oppose a state and not a society. 'We have no quarrel with the Afghan people,' the politicians dutifully avow, while striving to dismantle the existing political order of Afghanistan. This disavowal is not to be undervalued, despite its mantra-like character. Its meaning is that no society may try to prevent another from existing, nor from engaging in the normal self-sustaining activities of life: producing food, dwelling in houses, buying and selling, educating children, caring for the sick, publishing opinions, etc. Only when a society acts through its political and military structures in hostility to other societies may we take offence – at the hostility, that is, and not at the society's general functioning. Of course, the belligerent operations of a state depend on the smooth functioning of the society that supports them. If we were to deny our enemy the power to produce food, if we were to terrorise his market-places or flatten his residential suburbs, we might quite probably hamper his ability to pursue his wicked purposes against us; but such a route to victory is one we should deny ourselves, since it denies the right of peaceful social existence, a right in which we and our enemy both share. It manifests the antagonistic form that opposes *our* right to survive to *his* right to survive.

The rule, however, that the state and its organs are a legitimate target, is, as it stands, too rough. Not every operation of a government is hostile. It is reasonable, perhaps, to presume a certain unity in the operations of government; yet pictures of the wrecked Ministries of Justice and Local Government in Baghdad in 1991 naturally provoked the question what the rationale for attacking them had been. The administration of justice and of local government, though part of the state's operations, is not itself a threat to any other people. Similarly, attacks on post offices and telecommunications need to be justified by the presumption that military communications make use of them. The First Geneva Protocol forbids attacks on what it calls 'civilian objects', which it defines as objects which are not 'military objects' that 'by their nature, location, purpose or use make an effective contribution to military action'.[34] Much was heard in the course of the Gulf War about 'infrastructure targets', i.e., the network of communications – roads, power supplies, etc. – which facilitate the complexification of an economy. This same network probably serves to co-ordinate the military enterprise, and, if that is so, it becomes *prima facie* an object of attack. If direct material co-operation makes a legitimate target out of a person, direct military use makes a legitimate target out of a facility.

However, this *prima facie* justification may be overridden when the importance of the facility to the social fabric is so great that the military value of destroying it is incommensurate with the social damage it would do. Here the principle of proportion applies, to prevent an attack not of itself indiscriminate. Beyond the general principle above, the First Protocol extends special protection to 'cultural objects and places of worship', and to 'objects indispensable to the survival of the civilian population, i.e. foodstuffs, agricultural areas, crops, livestock, drinking-water installations and supplies and

---

[34] I Gen. Prot. 52–6 (Roberts and Guelff, eds, *Documents*, pp. 416–19).

irrigation works', which may not be attacked specifically with the purpose of denying their 'sustenance value' to the adverse party, unless they are used 'as sustenance only for armed forces' or 'in direct support of military actions' – provided, even so, that 'in no event shall actions . . . be taken which may be expected to leave the civilian population with such inadequate food or water as to cause its starvation or force its movement.' (To the evils which should not be encouraged to befall a civilian population, moreover, life-threatening epidemics should surely have been added.)

The final qualification, which makes the civilian need for food and water paramount over any military necessity, might helpfully have been set out as a separate clause, so that it did not depend on the specific purpose of denying 'sustenance value'. For other military purposes than that may prompt the destruction of installations essential to civilian life, as occurred in the course of the campaign against Baghdad, when much of the city lost its water-supply. This was due to allied attacks on water installations that had as their purpose not to deny immediate sustenance value, but to deny the power to generate electricity. Water-supplies are the paradigm for a socially essential infrastructure, which must take priority over the need to deny military use.

With these qualifications, nevertheless, the economic infrastructure, serving as it does both military and civilian use, is *prima facie* a legitimate object of attack. Not so the productive capacity of the economy itself. The traditional scorched-earth campaign, intended to deny the enemy the use of crops, was a common tactic of war; but burning of a crop does nothing to harm productivity, and may even improve it. Poisoning the land or its water-supplies, on the other hand, was categorically prohibited; for that would attack the very possibility of future cultural life in the region. In the same vein a famous text from the law of war in Deuteronomy protects fruit-trees in the course of a siege: 'When you besiege a city for a long time, making war against it in order to take it, you shall not destroy its trees by wielding an axe against them; for you may eat of them, but you shall not cut them down.'[35] That text invites some further reflections when it adds: 'Are the trees in the field men, that they should be besieged by you?' A direct attack on the non-human environment appears gratuitous in the course of a purely human struggle for justice. Can the whole earth, the presupposition of human life, be made victim to the need of human beings to render judgment on wrong? Such considerations, however, belong under the head of proportion rather than discrimination. When Iraq deliberately created an oil-slick in the Arabian Gulf in the course of the 1991 war, it was not, strictly speaking, an indiscriminate act, since it was aimed at allied naval operations. But the vast environmental damage incurred was disproportionate to its politico-military purpose.

Intention to distinguish

We come now to the second question: what does it mean to *intend* discrimination? Discrimination is from the start an intentional concept, and the development of just-war principles was at fault in trying to treat of a 'just intention' that was conceived as something different from it. There is, in fact, only one 'just intention' in armed conflict, and that is to distinguish innocence from guilt by overcoming direct co-operation in wrong. To search for a pure intention *behind* this intention is to chase a will o' the wisp. An act of war, like any other act, is inserted into a dense weave of practical purposes and intentions, most of which will inevitably be peculiar to the circumstance and the particular agents. Any one of these, if drawn out in such a way as to suggest that it is the 'real' purpose, can appear ulterior and irrelevant to the pursuit of justice, a corrupt motive undermining the moral pretensions of the enterprise. No one ever opposed a war without disclosing to the world that it had an ulterior motive which was its 'real' intention. Oil, it appears, is usually the favoured candidate.

---

[35] Deut. 20:19.

But the point is not that belligerent parties should have no further intentions or purposes. The point is that *this one* intention should shape the practical rationality of all that is actually undertaken in conflict, and that all other intentions should be subordinated to its demands and restraints.

The traditional formulation of the principle of discrimination requires that 'direct attack' should be restricted to combatant objects. It is not breached by the bare fact that non-combatants are killed, for it would require unusual conditions to avoid non-combatant casualties altogether. It is breached when they are attacked 'directly'. This distinction is valid for acts of judgment of every type, not only in armed conflict. When a man is sent to prison, a family is deprived of a father, a wife of a husband, perhaps elderly parents of a son, with consequences that may be the more terrible because they can be anticipated. Yet this is very different from the courts punishing families *directly*, by depriving relatives of convicted criminals of their jobs, for instance, as used to happen, we were told, in the Soviet Union. The indirect sufferings of non-combatants should figure in any estimation of the justice of an attack – but they belong under the heading of proportion, not of discrimination. Proportion is elastic, a matter of more or less. It makes sense to ask how many non-combatant casualties can be incurred without making the action disproportionate. It makes no sense to ask how many non-combatants may be attacked *directly*; for the answer is, not a single one.

The point which this traditional formulation leaves unclear is that 'direct' is an intentional notion. To attack any object 'directly' is to intend to damage it. 'Direct' material co-operation with wrong is to participate in acts which intend to damage what should not intentionally be damaged. The difference between 'direct' and 'indirect' damage, then, can be expressed as the difference between 'intended' and 'unintended' damage. The intention to damage only those forces that intend material co-operation with wrong is what makes an action discriminate; the intention to do any *other* damage is what makes an action indiscriminate, always remembering that the 'intention' in each case is not the whole range of purposes and motives that agents may bring to the act, but the practical rationality of the action itself.

As the traditional theory of double-effect well understood, it makes no moral difference to the intentional character of an act whether the harm is intended as an end or as a means. 'Regrettably,' the military spokesman may say, 'it has been necessary to eliminate the residential areas', and we rightly view him as a hypocrite, even though the regret may be perfectly genuine and the assault on non-combatants strictly necessary to the military purpose. Its necessity, indeed, was proof that it was intentional: the course of military action proposed would have been incoherent without it. The hypocrisy lies not in the feigning of regret, but in pretending that an intentional attack on non-combatants could be a matter for regret rather than repentance. A military purpose subject to such necessities should be abandoned. Quite differently from this, one may *foresee* damage to non-combatants, which is not intended as a means to the military purpose but cannot be avoided. The military goal does not imply the non-combatant damage, but the damage is an unavoidable ac-companiment to the pursuit of the goal. A military installation has to be disabled; this will involve damage to surrounding residential areas, but the damage contributes nothing as such to the disabling of the military installation. It is 'collateral', i.e., a 'side effect': it lies to one side of the path of means and ends which the intention is following.

This distinction, morally compelling as it is, has sometimes in-vited prevarication. The allied forces that bombed Hiroshima in 1945 claimed to have intended to destroy military installations; but had that been their true intention, they had other more suitable means at their disposal for doing so. A correct understanding of what intention means will allow an important corollary: the foresight that *dispropor-tionate* non-combatant damage will be done, combined with a *failure to intend to avoid* that disproportionate damage, presumes an inten-tion to do that damage. Foreseen damage is not as such intended; but when the foreseen damage is also gratuitous, it is presumed to be intended. So discrimination is not solely a matter of selecting a military object for attack, or simple 'targeting'. It is also a matter of attacking the target discriminatingly, i.e., proportioning the means to the object.

The most difficult practical dilemmas arising from this corollary concern aerial bombardment. 'Target-area bombing' is a name given to the prohibited practice of treating 'as a single military objective a number of clearly separated and distinct military objectives located in a city, town, village or other area containing a similar concentration of civilians or civilian objects'.[36] If the precise destruction of separate military targets requires separate attacks, one should not try to make do with one all-encompassing attack at a cost to non-combatant lives. For most practical purposes this rule makes excellent sense. Yet one could imagine circumstances of acute urgency which made the delay involved in separate attacks exceptionally perilous: for example, against separate missile launching sites, from any one of which an enemy might launch major attacks on centres of population. Urgency could make the separate destruction of each site impracticable; in which case the destruction of non-combatants would not be gratuitous; and if not gratuitous, not presumed to be intended; and if not presumed to be intended, genuinely collateral.

The point of noting such a possible exception is not to undermine a clear, and for almost all purposes binding, rule of warfare: don't attack targets where there are lots of non-combatants! It is to explore the *meaning* of the phrase 'intending harm to non-combatants' and to show why it is not synonymous with any other phrase, such as 'bombing cities', 'destroying residential areas', etc. One can test for the intention to harm non-combatants by putting a simple hypothetical question: if it were to chance that by some unexpected intervention of Providence the predicted harm to non-combatants did not ensue, would the point of the attack have been frustrated? If on 6 August 1945 all the citizens of Hiroshima, frightened by a rumour of what

---

[36] I Gen. Prot. 51.5 (Roberts and Guelff, eds, *Documents*, p. 416).

was to occur, had fled the city, would the attack have lost its point? If the answer is 'yes', then there was an intention to harm them, and their deaths were not collateral. If in the operation to separate the conjoint twins, Mary and Jodie, Mary's own heart and lungs had unforeseeably sprung to life as she was separated from Jodie's, and she had lived, would the operation have been deemed a failure? If the answer is 'no', Mary's death was collateral. The truly collateral damage in war is that which, if it could have been avoided, would have left the intended attack on a combatant object uncompromised. That is what is meant by calling it a 'side effect'.

To understand the intentional character of discrimination is to see how responsibility for discrimination may rest as much with the party attacked as with the party attacking. To locate potential combatant targets in deliberate proximity to non-combatant populations is to be guilty of those 'hostage shield' policies that have been such a deplorably constant feature of fighting in the Middle East. The First Geneva Protocol accordingly requires all parties to 'endeavour to remove the civilian population from the vicinity of military objectives' and to 'avoid locating military objectives in densely populated areas', as well as explicitly prohibiting 'human shield' policies to protect military installations.[37] Yet as we have seen, at the level of infrastructure targets, common to civilian and military uses, separation may be hard to achieve. If even post offices are legitimate targets because of their significance for military communications, not much separation from civilian centres of population can be looked for. It would be interesting to see a map of Britain indicating where we have located installations that were regarded as legitimate objects of attack in the bombing of Iraq, Bosnia and Afghanistan.

Nevertheless, such difficulties do not make the principle inoperable, and there are some flagrant breaches of it which must unquestionably be condemned. The tactics of guerrilla warfare raise the

[37] I Gen. Prot. 58; 51.7 (ibid., pp. 420, 416).

issue in its sharpest form, since they require the assimilation of fighting forces to the surrounding community. The enemy is permitted to move over friendly territory to an extent which would, in conventional warfare, secure victory, but continues to meet damaging opposition from forces camouflaged in the society around. Few types of warfare are so dreadful in their implications for non-combatants, who, precisely because they have daily contact with the enemy, are exposed to constant terror in order to secure their loyalty. The world community urgently needs humane conventions for the conduct of such struggles, which will allow more detachment on the part of non-combatants and will especially ensure the exclusion of children from armed combat.

Some thinkers have held that discrimination adds nothing significant to the principle of proportionate harm in governing the methods used in war. Are not all the restraints on warfare reducible to this one, that the extent of the harm we do should be justified by the extent of the threat we have to repel? They are not. Discrimination introduces an altogether more demanding restraint: it forbids us to aggregate damage done to non-combatants with damage done to combatants. In the eyes of God the soul of a soldier is of no less value than the soul of a milkman: why hesitate, we may wonder, to kill the milkman, if we do not hesitate to kill the soldier? But then, in the eyes of God the soul of a criminal is of no less value than the soul of an innocent citizen: why hesitate to imprison the innocent citizen, if we do not hesitate to imprison the criminal? In enacting judgment we are not invited to assume the all-seeing view of God, before whom no man living is justified, though we may never forget that God does, in fact, have that view. We have a specific *human* duty laid upon us, which is to distinguish innocence and guilt as far as is given us in the conduct of human affairs, not in order to put in question the equality of all human persons before God, but in order to respect the limits which God sets upon our invasion of other people's lives. To lose the will to discriminate is to lose the will to do justice.

4 Differences of proportion

Discrimination, we said, is an object of intention. To make a distinction between guilt and innocence is what defines the act of judgment and distinguishes it from any other kind of act. Proportion, on the other hand, has to do with the rational form which such an act assumes, i.e., with the shape of a successful act of judgment. The question of proportion has to be raised at two distinct points. On the one hand, since an act of judgment is reflexive, backward-looking, pronouncing on a preceding act or on an existing state of affairs brought about by previous acts or failures to act, it has to be proportioned by a truthful description of the wrong done. On the other hand, since an act of judgment is also forward-looking, constituting a law-governed context within which future acts, private or public, are to be performed, it must be proportioned to the state of affairs which it attempts to realise. In both retrospective and prospective aspects, then, as pronouncement and as lawgiving, the act of judgment must be shaped by rational proportion.

The tradition of the ethics of war has used the term 'proportion' largely in relation to the prospective aspect: an act of war is held disproportionate if the damage it does is excessive to the measure of peace it can reasonably hope to achieve. Looked at from this side, an act of judgment is proportionate in the same way as any other act may be: there is a prudent economy of expenditure and return. But looked at from the retrospective side, there is a distinctively judicial proportion to be observed, a responsibility to act in a way that reflects justly and truly on the nature and seriousness of the offence. This feature was treated by the tradition under the heading of 'just cause', and we shall address this aspect first, and at greater length.

Retrospective proportion

Vitoria proposed that there could only be one just cause for war, *iniuria accepta*, 'wrong done'; but he added that there were various legitimate objectives in war, the chief of which were a triad inherited from Roman law: to defend the public good, to reclaim losses and indemnify oneself, and to punish the wrongful aggressor.[38]

In saying, on the one hand, that the one just cause was 'wrong done', he meant to establish the character of war as judgment, a reactive pronouncement upon an offence, and so wrest armed force away from the antagonistic conception of self-defence. Anticipatory defence was ruled out. Premature military mobilisation grounded on suspicion was, the classic thinkers believed, one of the major sources of unnecessary and unjustified warmaking. Yet there was such a thing as a justified war of defence, distinguished from mere anticipation by the fact of actual, not merely possible, wrong. For Vitoria defensive war must be *in continenti*, in the emergency. For Suárez it was a response to wrong *in fieri*, actually being perpetrated.[39] This does not amount to endorsing the popular modern prejudice that a war is defensive if the other party fires the first shot. Suárez was aware of the possibility that 'an act may appear to be offensive, when it is defensive in fact'. Actual wrong can be perpetrated by other means than armed hostility, by economic strangulation, for example, or even by mere threat, since menace can constitute a decisive wrong in itself, even without being carried through.

Furthermore, a wrong may be actual even if it is only in preparation. *Iniuria accepta* does not have to be *iniuria perfecta*. To be the object of malicious preparation for war is already to be the victim of a wrong. Evidence of such preparation justifies defensive action, where mere suspicion does not justify it. So Grotius allowed defensive war against *iniuria non facta*, 'wrong not perpetrated', though with this strict qualification: 'The danger must be immediate . . . those who accept fear of any sort as a justification for preemptive slaughter are themselves greatly deceived and deceive others.'[40] This

---

[38] Vitoria, *De iure*, 1.3.13; 4.15–19, in *Political Writings*, pp. 303–4.

[39] Ibid., 1.2.5, in *Political Writings*, p. 300. Suárez, *De triplici virtute* 3.13.1 (*IG*, p. 737).

[40] Grotius, *De iure* 2.1.5, p. 172. Cf. 2.1.17: 'For protection against uncertain fears we must rely on divine providence and on a wariness free of reproach, not on force' (p. 183).

concession has an immediate bearing on the contemporary question of what we may do when we are presented with decisive evidence that a potential enemy is actively engaged in acquiring weapons of mass destruction.

Applying this restraint to modern conditions means insisting on the distinction between ordinary preparedness for defence, such as a state may maintain without any particular expectation of attack, and a prejudicial readiness for conflict which anticipates, rather than reacts to, indications of hostile intent. Not to be discouraged is a professionally competent and properly equipped standing army, for this avoids the need to recruit forces suddenly when a crisis looms, a measure which may itself be provocative in a tense situation; and it promises a more disciplined and controlled style of military action than one can expect from hastily trained conscripts or volunteers. The professional standing army has, of course, its dangers. Especially in states where political institutions are weak, a strong military class can form a rival focus of representation and have a destabilising effect.

But against this danger we must weigh the danger of the alternative which contemporary conditions too often create: dependence on too few soldiers and too many machines. The over-technologisation of the armies of the democratic West has tended to produce irresponsible military planning, and armed forces have sometimes come to seem more like minders of weapons-systems than guardians of international peace. Many of the morally disturbing features of the policies of NATO in the cold-war era were due to a combination of technical sophistication with chronic under-manning. For example, NATO could never renounce the nuclear first strike, since that was its only recourse in the event of a conventional attack which it was incapable of resisting by conventional means. Among the many complaints to be made about the forty-five-year-long cold war between Eastern and Western blocs, the way it encouraged prejudicial readiness for conflict was not the least serious: missile-launching systems with preselected targets were merely the symbol of a mindset in which the whole script for the next war was written in advance.

Nor, though it is difficult to separate fact from fiction, should we overlook the almost mythical expansion during that period of espionage, for the need to have detailed information of the enemy's military preparations is a need that belongs only to preparations for war. Classical just-war thinkers were very troubled by espionage, at least in so far as it implied the seduction of those who owed loyalty to their own peoples. Spies, they thought, should all be one's own nationals. Perhaps we will not take as seriously as they did the problem of treachery in open war. If there is a question of justice at issue and conscientious members of the enemy community decide that they cannot support their own state, why should we refuse their help? But in that case, of course, they are seeking the good of their own people, too. When there is no war, however, no promise of judgment to be rendered, no liberation to be effected, what is the common good for the sake of which we invite them to betray their people? It serves no concrete goal of justice, and the cause must be purely ideological. The 'idea' is at once the cause and the crime; espionage becomes more a tool of political philosophy than of political action. Satellite-based observance is a great improvement on massive espionage, since it simply extends the scope of public observation.

Within the single just cause, 'wrong done', there arises a variety of ways in which wrong may be complained of, and, correspondingly, a variety of ways in which the righting of wrong may be sought. In each instance there will be a particular description of the wrong, and this description will be reflected in the objectives which are framed. So those who undertake to perform judgment in war make themselves responsible for a certain articulate precision in the account they give of the wrong they propose to remedy, for the way the situation is described determines the shape of the enactment which may remedy it. 'Just cause', then, is not only a matter of concern at the beginnings of conflicts, but arises quite as pressingly with the question of when and how to end them. A cause can be exhausted when one has achieved all that it entitled one to do. If judgment has been enacted on the wrong complained of, there is no more judgment to be given. That does not mean, however, that those who resort to war should be able to foresee from the beginning exactly how far events will run, and know exactly where they will be required to stop. In the course of a war new crimes may be committed, new dangers emerge, which demand further action; the accomplishment of any war-aim has to be made safe by a settlement that it may take further pressure to achieve. The point is simply that what is *undertaken* must correspond to what is *purposed*, and what is *purposed* must correspond to what is reasonably *complained of*. That is what I mean by speaking of a 'descriptive' responsibility in shaping a strategy of war. 'Just cause' cannot be reduced to the mathematical (and mythological) point of overcoming evil as such.

The most interesting dilemmas about just cause in the Gulf War of 1991 arose in the closing stages of the campaign, when the allies had to decide whether they should do more than simply drive Iraq's forces from Kuwait. The alliance had never made the removal of the government of Iraq an aim of the war, though it was an avowed goal of policy on the part of some members. It might have been a justified war-aim, both in terms of defence (the subsequent crimes of the régime against its own Shiite and Kurdish populations caused many further headaches) and in terms of punishment, since the régime's already perpetrated crimes had richly justified its removal. But it was not practical to unite the alliance around such an aim, and once this fact was clear and agreed, the conduct of the war ought not to have been affected by it. The pounding of retreating troops on the Basra Road in excess of any tactical necessity, and the subsequent imposition of economic sanctions, were both defended as measures to hasten the fall of the régime. And though this may have been a legitimate goal of policy, it should not have been pursued *indirectly* by means of war, if it was not to be pursued *directly*.

The three traditional objectives of just war not only represent three different forms that an act of judgment may take, as punishment inflicted upon the forces of the offender, as defence in resistance to attack, and as reparation in the enforcement of a right; they also represent three elementary points of reference within the description of the wrong itself: the guilt of the offender, the peril of the victim, and the objective disorder in the sphere of right. So understood, it is plain that while these forms of judgment can be distinguished, they cannot be separated. Any concrete act of armed force will depend in some measure upon each of the three, and will combine defensive, reparative and punitive objectives, though with different weightings, depending on what the truth of the particular judgment requires. In any description of a wrong we must refer to the guilt of the offender, the danger the wrong poses, and the actual disorder effected. Each of these references is a necessary condition for establishing the fact of wrong done; and so each is a necessary element in the objectives for righting a wrong. A penal objective is necessary, because the other objectives do not of themselves impose a sufficiently restrictive limit to a belligerent power's ambitions. We need the idea of penal desert to restrict the potentially elastic permissions of defence and reparation. A defensive objective is necessary, because without real and pressing danger one cannot justify exposing the world to the dangers that war itself brings with it. A reparative objective is necessary, for without actual loss to be redressed the combination of malice and danger does not amount to an actual wrong.

However, the development of the doctrine of the three objectives has followed different lines. It has seemed possible to separate them concretely, so that one war may be identified as 'defensive', another as 'reparative' and a third as 'punitive'. This process was begun by Suárez in terms of the temporal relation of the just war to the wrong: the defensive war is undertaken simultaneously with the wrong, the other two subsequently. With the later degeneration of the tradition, however, and with the growth of the rights-tradition in its place, the distinction was seen more in terms of whose rights were at stake, one's own or other people's: defensive war was the pursuit of one's own rights, non-defensive war was intervention into another party's rights. Out of this problematic development there came an even more problematic turn in twentieth-century thinking about war, which was to consecrate the purely defensive war as the uniquely just war.

The tone of the modern doctrine is set by the Kellog-Briand Pact of 1928, in which the signatories condemned 'recourse to war for the solution of international controversies'. This phrase intended to exclude all war for positive (i.e., reparative or penal) purposes, and was quickly echoed in ecclesiastical circles, *e.g.* by the Lambeth Conference: 'The Conference affirms that war as a method of settling international disputes is incompatible with the teaching and example of our Lord Jesus Christ.'[41] After the Second World War the United Nations Charter forbade recourse to war on the part of any nation without explicit authorisation from the Security Council, but made an exception for a war of defence: 'Nothing in the present Charter shall impair the inherent right of individual or collective self-defence if an armed attack occurs against a member of the U.N., until the Security Council has taken measures necessary to maintain international peace and security.'[42] The thought of the Popes was running along parallel lines: Pius XII condemned 'aggressive' wars (using that term in a technical sense, to mean wars of reparation or punishment), and John XXIII condemned wars of reparation: 'It is hardly possible to imagine that in the atomic era war could be a fit means to restore violated rights.'[43] In forbidding non-defensive wars altogether, the

---

[41] Lambeth Conference 1930, resolution 25. The phrase became a favourite, echoed in 1948, 1958, 1968 and 1978, though it is not clear that its original meaning was remembered.

[42] Charter of the United Nations, 51, in Brownlie, *Basic Documents*, p. 13.

[43] Pius XII, Christmas Message 1944, in Michael Chinigo, ed., *The Teachings of Pope Pius XII*, London, Methuen, 1958; John XXIII, *Pacem in Terris: encyclical letter of Pope John XXIII on human rights and duties*, ed. Henry Waterhouse, London, Catholic Truth Society, 1980, 127. Pope John's words are highly ambiguous, to be sure, susceptible both of a pacifist reading – the original English translation rendered the phrase 'in defence of injured rights' – and of one which merely stresses the grave burden of proof that rests upon a claim to non-defensive intervention in the nuclear age.

Popes went further than the UN, which was content to restrict their authorisation.

But the attempt to privilege the defensive aim exclusively is a significant retreat from the spirit of the juridical proposal. It withdraws from the concept of an international community of right to the antagonistic concept of mortal combat; correspondingly, it is formally egoistic, protecting the rights of self-interest while excluding those of altruistic engagement. Furthermore, it encourages those who are inclined to war to be bold, by rewarding the surprise aggressor with secure tenure of his spoils and so providing an incentive to quick pre-emptive strikes. Its effects, in other words, are wholly demoralising.

The difficulty lies not with the notion that any just war must have a defensive rationale, which is clearly true, but with the notion that there can be an *exclusively* defensive rationale for a war, not associated with reparative or punitive aims. The apparent plausibility of the proposal arises from the multivocality of the term 'defence'. At the narrowest tactical level, 'defence' can refer to holding a line against attack; but since no war can be brought to a successful conclusion solely by operations of this kind, those who speak of 'defensive' war usually have in view a broader range of objectives, in which 'defence' can be distinguished from 'offence' (or, in the technical sense, 'aggression') as a protection of the *status quo*. Defence is resistance rather than an initiative, an opposition to enforced change. But at a yet broader level 'defence' may have the moral sense of securing injured right against wrongdoing. In this widest sense any war that is 'justified' is necessarily 'defensive' – but its defensiveness is simply a matter of relation to right; it is not opposed to 'aggression' in the technical sense of 'offence', but to 'aggression' in the moral sense we are more familiar with, i.e., wrongful injury. The point to grasp from all this is simply that a belligerent can be in a defensive posture *morally*, i.e., vindicating an injured right, while yet having *offensive* objectives, i.e., seeking to punish and to recover. And every just belligerent must in fact have *some* such offensive objectives.

Consider, for example, the case of a war of liberation. Here the reparative objective predominates. Wars of liberation aim to right past wrongs and reclaim lost liberties, overthrowing an unjust but established *status quo*. There are, of course, moral questions that arise about many such attempts. There can be more than a hint of inauthenticity about proposing to take up the wrongs of history, and it is downright mischievous to claim to inherit wrongs from ancestors when one lives under a régime that makes serious efforts to be just to all living parties. However, when such necessary reservations are made, it seems unthinkable to rule out wars of liberation *a priori*. Are subject populations long deprived of freedom to be told that they ought to have acted earlier if they were to act at all? The natural effect of attempting to suppress all but defensive wars is a tendency to stretch the time-frame of defence, in order to smuggle into it as many of the reparative objectives of war as possible. For Suárez, defence included no more than action taken to recover losses 'without noticeable delay'; that is to say, the wrongful attack can be considered *in fieri* if it has not yet confronted and survived a serious attempt to reverse it.[44] On this account the rescue of Kuwait in 1991, undertaken six months after its annexation by Iraq, was a defensive action, since the planning of armed resistance and the imposition of sanctions, which was the first act of war, all followed immediately upon the invasion, not to mention the fact that the invaders looted and destroyed their new possession, so prolonging the injury. But the US invasion of Panama in 1990, intended to restore power to the legitimate authorities many months after they were illegally deposed, would classically have counted as a war of reparation. This earlier incident illustrated another curious effect of the defence-only legal régime: if 'defence' is allowed no time-limit, it can be distinguished from other types of war only by conspicuous and pressing self-interest. So nations are forced to conceal altruistic or public-spirited grounds of action and

[44] Suárez, *De triplici virtute* 3.13.1 (*IG*, p. 737).

to make a parade of self-interest in order to qualify their actions as 'defensive'.

While reparative goals have tended to be colonised by increasingly self-referential notions of defence, another problem of intelligibility has arisen over the difference between reparative and punitive objectives. Here, of course, the general loss of intelligibility of punishment itself has been a complicating factor in a development that has gone astray in two directions. In the first place, notional separation of the 'reparative war' from the 'penal war' has created the impression that to punish is to do something *over and above* restoring the right, whereas to punish is in fact simply to restore the right, but to do it *with regard to* the guilt of the offender rather than the injury of the offended. The suppositious 'over and above' appeared unnecessarily moralistic, and so brought the notion of penal war into disrepute. In reaction to this the original distinction between penal and reparative war was lost sight of, and the two were bundled together into a category of 'offensive' war – a loss equivalent to the loss in domestic justice of a distinction between civil and criminal courts, in which all guilt would be 'liability'. But the notion of guilt was an important feature in the classical tradition, central to the analogy between domestic and international justice. When Vitoria, in his famous critique of the South American conquests, rejected the authority of the Pope to authorise penal interventions against unnatural crimes, he was careful not to reject altogether the idea of punishment in war. Punishment, he allowed, could justify wars of intervention where a society practised human sacrifice, cannibalism and tyrannical or oppressive acts.[45]

In our own time the notion of punishment, though hardly aired, is an important tacit support for wars of humanitarian assistance, for only penal desert can justify intervention into a foreign state's

---

[45] Francisco di Vitoria, *De Indis relectio* 2.5.40; 3.5.15, in *Political Writings*, pp. 273–5, 287–8.

jurisdiction and taking responsibility out of its hands. Without it, international justice is pushed back upon the 'perimeter fence'. But the notion also has a critical rôle in keeping war objectives limited. The pursuit of safety can run to indefinite lengths, and the pursuit of right without regard to guilt can be a cruel thing. When Palestinian guerrillas cross the border from the Occupied Territories into Israel and perform isolated acts of terrorism, in reprisal for which Israel launches massive artillery bombardment, we call it 'over-reaction'. What we mean is simply that there is a *penal* disproportion between offence and response. Whatever the guilt of the attack, it strikes us that the Palestinians have 'not deserved' all that they are forced to take. Israel may appeal to its need for safety; but that need is infinitely elastic. To require a penal objective guards against the resort to war as a response to non-culpable injury, and prevents the subtle expansion of defensive war-aims into further goals, such as colonisation. Common prejudice is inclined to suppose that punitive objectives make for unbridled war; but the truth is more or less the opposite: they impose the tightest of reins, since punishment is measured strictly by desert.

Prospective proportion

With this we come to discuss the forward-looking aspect of proportion, its fitness to achieve a rationally desirable state of affairs. Forward-looking justifications of acts of judgment can sometimes be taken for granted. With an act of judgment performed by a court, for example, we can usually concentrate our questions on its retrospective proportion, and assume that if all is in order there, it is bound to serve the common good well enough, since court judgments serve the common good simply by upholding the law. But with other types of judgment, it is not so easy. An act of legislation requires a forward-looking justification in terms of a predictable improvement in the legal régime. With judgment by armed conflict the requirement of prospective proportion is even more pressing, since it is a venture outside the given spheres of government, and the only means available run the risk of a breach in the banks of practical rationality that could release a flood of absolute antagonism. So the principle that erects a barrier against 'cruelty of revenge, implacable hostility, savagery in retaliation'[46] – rejecting, in other words, the ecstatic logic of mortal conflict and requiring prospective proportion for every use of force – is of critical importance in imposing the rationality of an act of judgment in warfare.

The end to which an act of judgment must be proportioned is a political end. That is to say, it must achieve *peace*, understanding that term properly to include all that is comprised in a stable and settled political order, including the justice and law-governed character of relations established within it. 'Victory', as such, is not a political end, not a state of society which one can reasonably and responsibly pursue. It is a purely military term, referring to the position in which enemy forces are permanently denied effective or useful movement. Nor is victory even a universally necessary means to attaining a political end through war; whether it is necessary or not in any given case depends on whether peace can be made first, before either side achieves a victory. Military decision-making aims at victory, because that is according to its military logic; but military decision-making must be subject to political decision-making, and political decision-making aims only at peace. To require prospective proportion in any act of war is to require that it be serviceable not only to victory but to peace.

The difficulty in practice is that the peace which any conflict aims at is still indeterminate, known only negatively as the correction of the grave injustice that afforded the cause. From this it follows that there is more than one point of reference in relation to which proportion may be assessed. The two traditional principles of 'last resort' and 'prospect of success', for example, identify two different ways of proportioning an action in relation to its end: the one comparing it

---

[46] Thomas Aquinas, *Summa Theologiae* 2-2.40; Blackfriars edn pp. 80–5.

with alternative possible courses of action, the other measuring the risks of failure. On the one hand, assuming that armed conflict must in general be the worst method of effecting a political judgment, we are expected to exhaust all other possibilities before resorting to it. On the other hand, we are required to weigh up whether failure, or likely damage, would be so great as to render the attempt self-defeating. Thus two possible sins against practical rationality are identified and warned against: a precipitate rush to arms, and a stubborn refusal to count the cost. But neither of these warnings must always have the final word. They can only support *prima facie* cases against resort to war, cases which may in a particular instance be trumped by broader prudential considerations.

So, as we learned in 1991, we may have to cut short the glimmer of a hope of negotiated solution if negotiations are deliberately dragged out to shorten the campaigning season and render the chances of effective military action nugatory. The 'last' resort is bounded by the last practicable moment for effective action. Or we may have to accept hazardous risks, if the consequences of inaction are likely to be more hazardous still. An adversary far advanced on the road towards biological weapons is worth a very great deal more loss to stop than one who presents no comparable hazard. The 'reasonable' prospect of success is determined by what reason prompts in the light of real and present danger. It does not rule out the need to take risks. So judgments of proportion have an uncertain predictive character to them; yet that does not mean that no judgment of proportion can ever be decisive. The situation may arise in which we can only judge that beginning or prolonging, or *not* beginning or *not* prolonging, an armed struggle for justice would be gravely imprudent – and if gravely imprudent, then wrong.

Proportion is, indeed, *always* the decisive argument in bringing conflict to an end: one side has to reach the unilateral judgment that there is nothing to be gained from further fighting, either because so much has been gained already, or because so much has been lost.

Any conflict undertaken as a proportionate means to the end of just peace will become disproportionate in the end, by virtue of one of two facts: it will have failed, or it will have succeeded. Either way it will have become superfluous to any political goal. Those, then, who like to employ the categories of just war solely to disallow every attempt at judgment by armed conflict, know what they are about when they they take their stand each time on the ground of disproportion. Like the stopped clock which is sure to tell the correct time twice in twenty-four hours, they only have to go on saying that it is disproportionate for long enough, and sooner or later events will catch up with them!

With regard to the question of the proportion of acts *in* war, we find the classic just-war thinkers asserting the disconcertingly open-ended thesis that anything necessary to the prosecution of a war justly undertaken may be done.[47] Read with the requisite emphasis on the word 'necessary', this offers the simplest formulation of the criterion of proportion as such: that destructive measures must not outrun the requirements of establishing peace. Such a principle raises in the first place a series of questions about tactical and logistical prudence, not to be ignored despite their largely technical character. But behind these there are wider questions about what measures secure *peace*, as opposed to merely securing *victory*. We need professional soldiers to ensure that the first range of questions is properly addressed; but we need our soldiers to be answerable to politicians, in order that the second range of questions, too, should be properly addressed.

The 'strategic studies' which became a respectable, even fashionable, intellectual pursuit in the days of the cold war demonstrate what goes wrong when military prudence supplants political prudence. Formalistic doomsday scenarios, discussions of how to win the next nuclear war without forfeiting the conditions to fight the next nuclear war but one, and so on, tossed around an abstract idea

---

[47] Vitoria, *De iure* 1.4.15, in *Political Writings*, p. 304.

of victory that had no relation at all to what is required of the world for it to be a habitable place for human communities. Prosecuting an act of judgment in armed conflict means strengthening the conditions for justice in and among human communities; it cannot mean overthrowing those conditions. War is a race in which there is no guarantee that either contestant will cross the finishing-line; knocking the opponent out does not constitute success in the sense that really matters. An act of war, then, may be disproportionate even if it ensures victory, and even if nothing less would have ensured victory; for it may frustrate the very object for which the conflict was joined in the first place.

This has obvious implications for methods of fighting and types of armament. Any mode of combat which is likely to inflict grave damage on a society's capacity – including the enemy's capacity – to return to a state of ordered justice falls under this general condemnation. Of course, a war may be excused considerable damage to the peace and justice of society if, had the enemy prevailed, the damage would have been much worse; a Europe wholly subject to the rule of Nazism was an evil worth some significant loss to avert. Methods of conflict, too, therefore, may expand upwards on the scale of destructiveness in proportion to the scale of the threat they are likely to meet.

Nevertheless, there comes a point at which methods of combat reach such a pitch of destructiveness that they simply cease to offer proportionate defence in any conceivable circumstance, since any use of them will destroy, more or less without remainder, the good that it purported to save. Proportion is an elastic concept, but not indefinitely elastic. There is such a thing as a *categorically* disproportionate means of combat, one which would be inappropriate to meeting any threat whatever. To be convinced of this, we do not have to determine precisely where the line of categorical disproportion is to be drawn; we only have to identify some case that lies beyond it. Shall I, perhaps, command agreement, if I repeat a suggestion I have made elsewhere, that anyone who reflects on the certain consequences (ignoring, for the sake of the argument, the very many uncertain ones) of exploding 6.33 megatons simultaneously in two hundred cities – which was believably said to be NATO's war-fighting plan for a nuclear engagement with the Warsaw Pact – will know immediately that no imaginable good could ever be served by such a measure?[48]

[48] Cf. *Peace and Certainty*, p. 17.

2 | Counter-insurgency war

Within the general class of civil – or, as it is usually called today, 'internal' – armed conflict there is a special problem with insurgency campaigns waged by non-governmental armies that, sometimes by choice but often by necessity, pursue a strategy of disseminating active armed units invisibly through the civil population. This puts the whole population in the position of a hostage shield, compelling a conventional military response to incur high levels of non-combatant damage – and adding insult to injury, no doubt, by exploiting the damage subsequently for propaganda purposes. The first moral question that arises from this practice is how counter-insurgency force can operate effectively while maintaining a respect for discrimination which insurgency does not share.[1] But there is a second question, which I shall pursue in the reflections that follow. That is, can the conduct of counter-insurgency be conducted in such a way as to persuade insurgents to abide by the principle of discrimination?

The strategy of penetrating the civil population is already different from 'terrorism'. The terrorist makes his point by slaughtering the innocent intentionally; the insurgent makes his by forcing his opponent to slaughter the innocent unintentionally. Insurgents may

---

[1] The pioneering discussion was that of Paul Ramsey's 1966 article, prompted by the Vietnam War, 'How shall counter-insurgency war be conducted justly?', in *The Just War*, New York, Scribners, 1969, pp. 427–64. Ramsey asked: 'Can counter-insurgency abide by the distinction between legitimate and illegitimate military objectives while insurgency deliberately does not?' (433). In the present discussion the focus of the question is slightly different: can the conduct of counter-insurgency hostilities ever succeed in *persuading insurgency forces, too,* to abide by such a distinction?

also be terrorists in fact; in the public mind, understandably enough, they are so almost by definition. Yet the difference is not to be dismissed lightly; every step towards restraint gains some ground for the civilising of armed conflict. To the extent that insurgents desist from immediate acts of terror, they display a higher level of respect for the demands of justice, even if their exploitation of the civil population as hostages fails to display respect at a very high level.

But is that the *only* restraint of which an insurgent force is capable? Granted that the dissemination of forces through the civil population is an unavoidable strategy for a revolutionary struggle, could other restraints or rules of conduct be applied to it, without frustrating the whole enterprise of insurgency warfare? From the point of view of the populations affected by such strife it is in the highest degree desirable that further restraining conventions should be devised and observed. But inventing rules for guerrilla armies to keep looks like a fool's game. Revolutionary war is prohibited by every national jurisdiction, and hostage-shield strategies are prohibited by international law. What, we may wonder, could be achieved by further multiplying formal prohibitions?

For this reason the reflections of the international legal community turned towards the possibility of providing an incentive, which might attract those waging war against governments to observe further disciplines and restraints. It was thought at first that the offer of prisoner-of-war status for captured fighters would be incentive enough. The alternative for the illegal combatant was to be shot, or more humiliatingly hanged, after the most summary of legal processes.[2] As early as the Fourth Hague Convention of 1907 it was seen that this incentive could fruitfully be extended to certain 'irregular' militias to persuade them to conduct themselves appropriately on the battlefield. The privileges of prisoner-of-war status were opened to forces commanded by a person responsible for his subordinates,

[2] A tradition more or less forgotten in recent times, until recalled in 2001 by the US government, which hoped to classify foreign al-Qaeda fighters in Afghanistan as illegals.

wearing an identifying emblem distinguishable at a distance, carrying arms openly, and conducting their operations in accordance with the law of war.[3] These provisions had in mind unruly militias, independent of national armies, which participated in an otherwise conventional war. In the Third Geneva Convention of 1949 the net was cast still wider, to include 'organised resistance movements', i.e., those fighting against a government that claimed to exercise jurisdiction over them.[4] And then in the First Geneva Protocol of 1977 a dramatic insertion into a late draft made the provisions of that document apply to 'peoples fighting against colonial domination and alien occupation and against racist regimes in the exercise of their right of self-determination'.[5] Two further provisions made it easier to qualify for recognition. One relaxed the demand for an identifying emblem, 'recognising . . . that there are situations in armed conflicts where, owing to the nature of the hostilities, an armed combatant cannot so distinguish himself', and required only that fighters should carry arms openly in military engagements and preparatory deployments. The second allowed the authority representing a people engaged in armed conflict of this type to act unilaterally to apply the provisions of the Protocol to bind not only itself but its colonial, occupying or racist oppressors.[6]

The tendency in international law, then, has been to expand the status and conditions governing irregular troops to include resistance movements, relaxing the rules somewhat to accommodate to their different circumstances, all with the idea of tempting such movements to sign up to international norms of conduct. Civilian populations will benefit if this is successful, for insurgents will have to respect their immunity from attack, and will be weaned away from the hostage-shield and terrorist tactics. And it has been supposed

---

[3] 1907 Hague Convention IV Regulations 1. In Adam Roberts and Richard Guelff, eds, *Documents on the Laws of War*, 2nd edn, Oxford, Oxford University Press, 1989, p. 48.

[4] 1949 Geneva Convention III a4. Ibid., p. 218.

[5] 1977 Geneva Protocol I a1. Ibid., p. 390.

[6] a44, ibid., pp. 411f.; a96, ibid., pp. 443f.

that revolutionary forces themselves will benefit, by being rewarded for their restraint with prisoner-of-war status, which implies relative immunity from interrogation and prosecution, as well as recognition of their representative status. The losers, it has been assumed, are governments, since their prerogative of suppressing rebellion by all means permitted in domestic law is inhibited by international law.

In keeping with this assumption the British government entered a series of reservations when it signed the 1977 Geneva Protocols, tending to resist the inclusion of terrorist organisations within the scope of the provisions. 'Armed conflict,' it said, 'implies a certain level of intensity of military operations' and should not cover 'isolated and sporadic acts of violence'. The privileges afforded to resistance movements must apply only in 'occupied territory', or in struggles that genuinely fit the description afforded in article 1: 'peoples fighting against colonial domination and alien occupation and against racist regimes in the exercise of their right of self-determination'. Furthermore, the authority which has the right to bind its opponent to the provisions of the Protocol should be 'recognised as such by the appropriate regional inter-governmental organisation' – a very restrictive condition indeed, requiring (let us say) ETA to get official recognition from the European Union before it can bind Spain to treat its captives as prisoners of war. To come under the laws of war, in other words, it is not enough to think of *yourselves* as freedom fighters; you must be recognised by everybody as the representatives of an enslaved or occupied population.[7] Correspondingly, Western societies have thought it better to pursue their struggles against the less deserving class of insurgents (i.e., those that arise in the Western democracies) by means of the criminal law. The European Convention on the Suppression of Terrorism (1991) attempted to 'ensure that effective extradition arrangements are in place in relation to all such crimes', denying those accused of terrorist

---

[7] Ibid., pp. 467f.

offences the benefit of the immunity usually accorded to political offences.[8]

The suggestion is worth entertaining, however, that this general assumption about the relative benefits of irregular-fighter status is no longer valid. The alternative faced by armed militias in 1907 was to be strung up from the nearest tree or lamppost. Today revolutionary fighters in an otherwise peaceful society face a criminal process cumbrous for government but offering welcome publicity to the cause, strung out by appeals and agitations for review, all offering further political benefits, and resulting, in the most favourable case, in acquittal for lack of criminal evidence, or, in the least favourable, a decade or two of imprisonment such as would allow a young man an opportunity to begin his life again at forty. Arguably, there is simply not enough to deter a determined insurgency force from acts of terrorism, and no incentive to reward restraint. It could possibly be in the interest not only of non-combatants but also of governments to remove such conflicts from the criminal sphere and put them on a war footing. But that needs more deterrent and more incentive. The stick and the carrot must be applied to the correct ends of the animal.

Consider, as a test-case for this suggestion, the long and exhausting quarter-century of struggle on the part of the two governments of Britain and Ireland to overcome the IRA. Excluded from the protections, but also from the demands, of the law of war, active members of the IRA, when captured, were treated in both states as criminals. This had at least three troubling implications. First, there was no incentive for the IRA to bring their struggle to an end, politically static though it was; the advantage always lay with making one further attempt, and nothing was to be gained from stopping. Secondly, there was no incentive for them to desist from acts of terror against the civil population. As a matter of fact, there were periods in which the IRA, seeking legitimacy for its organisation and its struggle,

[8] http://stars.coe.fr/ta/ta91/EREC1170.HTM.

imposed upon itself some of the rules of military combat, directing attacks on what it understood to be legitimate targets. Its restraint in these periods won it no reward; and when it reverted to terrorist acts, it incurred no additional penalty. Thirdly, and most seriously, the criminal courts in Britain and in Ireland were unable to deal properly with the charges brought before them. The standards of proof required in a criminal prosecution were too high, the labour of preparing prosecutions too long and too detailed, the process of detection on an incident-by-incident basis too minute, to allow an effective response to an organised campaign of war. Furthermore, the system of criminal justice itself became corrupted by the effort to cope with something it was never designed for. In Ireland there was the unhappy vacillation of courts over politically unpopular laws on extradition. In Ulster there was the era of special courts, designed to remove the trial of terrorist offences from the vagaries of the jury system – a solution which failed to satisfy the expectations of criminal justice without guaranteeing counter-terrorist efficiency. And in mainland Britain there was deep corruption of the courts by fabricated prosecution evidence, gravely weakening public confidence in the police.

Within any civil community a situation may arise in which civil order is confronted with defiance too great to overcome by normal judicial processes. In December 1989, while everything was happening in Central Europe, the following news story crept out almost unnoticed from Colombia. Seventeen-year-old Fredy Gacha, released from jail at the end of a short term in November, was secretly trailed by a thousand police and marines until unwittingly he led them to the headquarters of his father, drug baron Rodriguez Gacha, in the midst of the jungle. The forces closed in and gunned down Fredy, his father and their retainers as they attempted to escape. There was no legal process; it was a simple act of war, even though directed against citizens. To understand the reasons that could have led to it, one must appreciate the damage done to judicial process and civil order in Columbia by the drug cartels. A justification could only be framed on the basis of necessity: that it would have invited disaster to have attempted to bring such a figure to trial in open court.

Such necessities do not arise, of course, without a serious decay in governmental authority. But governmental authority is God's will for human communities, and should, as such, be strengthened. Not always strengthened precisely on its existing foundations, of course, since it may have contributed to its own decay by failing to represent the people well or by failing to satisfy the demands of justice. But some centre of authority must be located and defended; and that means on the one hand enhancing the representative character of government, and on the other strengthening its imposition of justice. The strategy for counter-revolutionary warfare, then, must be twofold: (a) straightforward and effective resistance to the violent threat to civil authority; (b) political adjustment, to the extent that this will facilitate a more durable and representative governmental authority. There can be no general rule as to how much political concession and how much forceful resistance is appropriate, for that depends on the scope of revolutionary demands, the extent of their support in the community, and so on. But inasmuch as it is an association of political revolution that has to be engaged with, there will need to be concessions that should not be made to criminals; and there will need to be direct force that should not be used against criminals.

Resistance to insurgency is something different from conventional international war, because the two communities are interdistributed over the same space; but it is also different from the enforcement of criminal justice. The rules that govern it are bound to be a hybrid of rules for civil justice and rules for war. But a hybrid is the result of a *positive* conjunction of the principles governing each parent-type. Counter-insurgency law is not situated in a vacuum in between the two legal systems, a sphere of 'neither . . . nor . . .'.[9] If we are to

---

[9] At this point I find a weakness in the approach of E. Gross, 'Self-defence against terrorism: what does it mean? the Israeli perspective', *Journal of Military Ethics* i(2),

conceive of a *law* that governs insurgency and counter-insurgency operations, we must draw analogies from existing legal thinking. Let us, then, pursue a thought-experiment as to what might be implied in a counter-insurgency strategy which drew significantly upon the law and morality of war. The moralist enjoys a happy liberty to conduct thought-experiments that might run into difficulties in practice, and we will not worry too much about the modalities of ours. Yet, if they are to be at all illuminating, such experiments cannot be simply *unrealistic*. They must be framed for the world as we know it, and not some other world; and their virtue must lie in exposing the moral logic of different strategies of action that could be adopted within the world as we know it. The purpose of the following speculation, then, is to discover what would be implied if civilised societies began to think of insurgency movements as their opponents in war rather than as gangs of criminals.

In the first place, such an analogy would require a greater discrimination to be introduced into the *agencies* of force brought to bear against an insurgent enemy. If the enemy is to be persuaded to observe the rule of discriminate attack, counter-insurgency forces must be distinguished from ordinary agencies of government. When local volunteer militia, regular police and criminal courts pursue, prosecute and try revolutionaries, all those institutions become legitimate targets for attack. Even while the IRA practised a policy of discrimination, judges were shot dead sitting by their firesides with their children, off-duty policemen were gunned down as they left church, and so on. These distressing scenes could not simply be blamed upon the heartlessness of the revolutionary fighters; they were a natural

---

2002, 91–108, an article that correctly identifies the *problem* about handling counter-terrorist operations under the internal law of states. But, beside the fact that the author fails to distinguish insurgents from terrorists, he defines the space for a law of war against terrorism wholly negatively: 'terrorists are not entitled to the broad protection given to civilians, and they are also not combatants . . .' (94). This leaves him without the necessary points of reference to control a train of thought based wholly on national self-defence.

THE JUST WAR REVISITED

consequence of the policy of integrating counter-revolutionary resistance into the fabric of the criminal law. IRA decisions about what
constituted legitimate targets were sometimes wilful (as when they
attacked tradesmen who dealt with the army in routine business), but
many of their targets could be defended as materially co-operating
with counter-insurgency hostilities. The implication of a war-based
strategy would have been that operations against the IRA would have
been entrusted to distinct military forces based in well-defended
barracks; and that trials, where necessary, would be conducted (as
required by the Third Geneva Convention on prisoners of war) by
military courts.

Precisely this point was the focus of a much-discussed disagreement between the Irish and the British governments. The Irish urged
that police should always accompany the army on routine patrols,
a policy clearly intended to reinforce the criminal paradigm. The
British government had reservations about the idea, and was right
to have them, though it failed to draw the obvious conclusion: that
the criminal-law paradigm was the wrong one to apply. It could do
no good to convert the police into agents of war; for that could only
undermine their civil authority over the non-combatant Republican
community. The reason for the Irish government's mistaken attitude
was, however, instructive. Viewed by republican militias as having no
legitimacy as the government of Ireland, it had much more pressing
reasons than its British counterpart to make the *political* gesture of
denying all shred of legitimacy to the IRA (which, after all, never
questioned the British government's right to rule the island of Great
Britain!). But this reasoning wrongly imposed political concepts of
legitimacy upon decisions about military operations. To conduct
hostilities in a way that treated the IRA as an *army* was not the same
thing as to recognise them as a legitimate *political* force. To accept
that the confrontation was a military one, and that the force to be
overcome was a military force that must be overcome by military
means, was not to warrant any concession to the bizarre political
mythology that the IRA took the field to promote. There can, after

all, be such a thing as a civil war, in which two sides compete for an indivisible political legitimacy. The essential difference between a gang of criminals and an insurgent army is simply that the latter can count upon a wider supportive community, in relation to which it occupies something of a representative rôle. Where such a community exists, and inter-communal enmity is woven into the fabric of society, it does no good at all to ignore the fact, and to pretend that it is not civil strife but merely criminality that has to be overcome.

In the second place, the analogy could not be pressed to the point of insisting on the rule that revolutionary fighters must carry arms openly to qualify for POW status. This rule seems to fall uncomfortably between two stools. On the one hand it does not offer enough protection to non-combatants in the event of open exchange of fire, a situation which requires both parties to be identified by uniform or identifying emblem, if combatants are to distinguish each other from bystanders. Such operations, however, do not often involve exchange of fire, and it surely imposes too grave a burden on those engaged, let us say, in planting a bomb in a military post, that they should place the bomb openly on the back seat of their car as they go! Nothing would be lost for counter-terrorist effectiveness if this rule were waived, though retaining, perhaps, full uniform requirements for operations involving certain types of weapon suited principally for open attack on armed troops.

In the third place, however, the analogy would require that expectations for the treatment of enemy combatants would correspond more closely to those of military law rather than to those of criminal law. This has implications both for prisoners' liability to execution and for the terms on which prisoners are held.

In conventional war the power to take and hold prisoners is derived from the power to kill the enemy combatant who does not surrender. The two powers go together and support each other. A prisoner of war who conspires to escape or to make war from within the place of imprisonment is liable to summary execution. In insurgency and counter-insurgency war, however, the powers of death and the power of restraint are separated. The insurgent militia, if it employs guerrilla tactics, has a virtual monopoly of the power to kill, for it is not often that an active unit will get squarely within its opponents' sights; while counter-insurgency, in countries where the criminal law has renounced the death penalty for murder, is largely dependent upon arrest and imprisonment. This is one of the unsatisfactory features of counter-revolutionary strategies in liberal societies. The very disequilibrium may tempt security forces to resort to murder rather than entrust their adversaries to the over-tender care of the criminal justice system. Precisely this argument, in fact, has been used in support of Israel's controversial policy of the official assassination of Palestinian leaders.[10] I assume, however, that there are good reasons for the disapproval in which the assassination of war leaders is held in the customary law of war: on the one hand, it lacks the degree of public accountability that is present even in a summary trial, and so fails to conform to the essential conditions of an act of judgment; on the other, it attacks war leaders as individuals rather than through the militias of which they are the representatives.

A change of strategy would demand some restoration of the equilibrium. On the one hand, revolutionary forces would be expected to take prisoners, and not merely to kill. That principle is as fundamental as desisting from attack on non-combatants, and it would be all-important to have it recognised. International supervision could then be called upon to ensure the detention of prisoners in proper conditions. On the other, the question would have to arise about the use of the death penalty by military (not civilian) courts, to provide a sanction against breach of the laws of war by indiscriminate or perfidious acts. This would allow for the execution of those who performed acts of terror against non-combatants, who performed acts of war without due identification from a revolutionary militia, or who abused the terms of their detention to continue hostilities.

[10] See ibid.

Using analogies drawn from the law of war, the circumstances of those held prisoner could be considerably improved, especially if the full resources of international co-operation and oversight were secured. The offices of the International Committee of the Red Cross would presumably be available; but in the context of internal struggles there could be a specially valuable rôle for a device envisaged by the 1949 Geneva Conventions, but little used: that of an independent Protecting Power to act on behalf of each party, safeguarding the interests of its personnel. If such a Power would accept its party's prisoners on its own territory, they could be effectively removed from the scene of conflict, and so enabled to live under a more relaxed régime. Here again the customary principles governing domestic justice and those governing the conduct of war lead us in opposite directions. With criminal justice it is assumed that imprisonment should be within the general locality of the prisoners' home, to facilitate contacts with family; but with prisoners of war the expectation is that they will be detained away from the combat zone, for reasons of their own safety.[11] Distance is an obvious advantage in the case of internal strife, since the presence of politically motivated prisoners within the community affected can only exacerbate the political problems, and requires immense and oppressive security arrangements. The conversion of prisons in Northern Ireland into armed fortresses is an example of how ineptly criminal-law expectations accord with the realities of armed conflict, and it can hardly have assisted the welfare of those detained there. Distance, especially if it could be measured in thousands of miles, would allow for a more open régime than that envisaged in the Geneva Conventions, one which might even be reduced to passport control and travel restrictions, allowing prisoners of war to enjoy something like a normal life, not excluding (if desired) being joined by members of their families. There is, however, a less radical possibility that is also worth entertaining: to re-introduce the status of political prisoner into our existing system of criminal

---

[11] 1949 Geneva Convention III a19. Roberts and Guelff, *Documents*, p. 224.

detention, a provision traditional in many other countries with other legal systems. The prisoner who enjoys political status is usually allowed a more relaxed prison régime.[12]

What, then, would everybody gain by such a change of strategy? – for without a general incentive to adopt it, it is hardly worth speculating about. For the government there would be an intelligence gain: the revolutionary forces would be required to identify their soldiers – perhaps simply by public acknowledgment of them after arrest or perhaps by identification cards carried on their persons, as required of combatants in conventional war.[13] Once identified, they could be detained for the duration of the conflict without further criminal process. This is not 'internment', which is a preventive measure, but detention of those acknowledged as enemy combatants. What the revolutionary army would gain would be immunity from interrogation after arrest and a measure of formal recognition. What the individual insurgent would gain would be the comparative security and liberty of POW status under international supervision. What the non-combatant population would gain would be an incentive to the militias to conduct their operations discriminatingly. And what everyone would gain would be an increasing pressure to settle, as the number of prisoners of war increased, waiting upon a formal cessation of hostilities for their release. There would be corresponding losses: to the government, of information gained by interrogation; to the insurgent militias, of the opportunity to deny involvement and to hope for an acquittal in the criminal court. The viability of a change of strategy would depend on the gains seeming to outweigh the losses for both combatant parties. No party could impose it one-sidedly.

So much for our thought-experiment, which has aimed simply to delineate the peculiar difficulties of applying law to the fighting of wars of insurgency. The constructive point that should not be

---

[12] The status existed notionally in English law until 1972, and allowed a régime like that afforded to prisoners on remand and awaiting trial. In Northern Ireland there was a comparable provision for 'special category' prisoners between 1972 and 1976.

[13] 1949 Geneva Convention III a17. Roberts and Guelff, *Documents*, p. 223.

forgotten is this: anyone who fights a war of any kind, insurgency or counter-insurgency included, has a duty so to act as to bring it to an end within a reasonable time-scale, whether by victory or by concession. The tragedy of internal conflicts fought by guerrilla methods is that they are unending. Neither side is capable of inflicting such damage on the other as to create a real and urgent will for settlement. The virtue of taking prisoners of war rather than imprisoning criminals is that it brings to bear upon both parties an increasing pressure to settle generated by a growing colony of exiled prisoners, waiting upon the conclusion of hostilities for the opportunity to resume their normal lives at home. 'Prisoner release' was a major part of the package that secured the Good Friday Agreement in Northern Ireland. It was, of course, widely criticised by Unionists on the ground that amnesties of that kind were no part of the lawful treatment of criminals. Precisely!

3 | Immoral weapons

The traditional concerns of moral reflection about war have been with the causes for which wars are begun and the methods by which they are conducted. Neither of these trains of thought can lead us directly to any conclusion about the instruments with which war is practised or prepared for. To speak of proportion and discrimination is to speak of ways of acting; but instruments are apparently adaptable to different ways of acting. The surgeon's scalpel can be used to commit murder, the pirate's cutlass to perform a surgical operation. It may seem, then, as though the contemporary concern over types of weapons can have no purchase in the traditional moral categories of intention and action. If instruments are neutral, what could possibly be said in general terms about the morality of different types of weapon, which might be used for moral or immoral purposes depending on those who used them?

But this doubt need not delay us long. If a scalpel can be used to commit a murder and a cutlass to perform an amputation, that does not mean there is no moral significance in the difference between the two implements. A surgeon's scalpel on the steward's requisition list for a merchant vessel would cause nobody any alarm; two dozen cutlasses might. The point is commonly made that instruments are designed in relation to purposes, and bear within their design the purposes they were conceived for. The form which weapons take tells us what kind of fighting is envisaged. The peculiar weapons of our age give voice to certain hypothetical war plans and are open to criticism inasmuch as the plans themselves are open to criticism.

There is, however, one point that must be conceded to the theory of neutrality, misleading as it is. New uses may be found for weapons that were designed for immoral tasks. The prophets of ancient Israel envisaged a day when swords might be adapted to an agricultural function; and without looking quite that far ahead, we can well see how parts of a weapons system designed for total-war use could be kept in readiness for just-war use, at least until some more appropriate elements could be devised. Delivery systems are an obvious example of this. Multiple Independent Re-entry Vehicles, designed to enhance the totality and indiscriminacy of a nuclear attack, can be put to use with conventional warheads in the so called 'carpet bombing' of troops. We must, then, admit the flexibility of instruments as a factor in our thinking; but that does not invalidate the question of what weapons are unsuited to just-war strategies.

Objections raised against particular types of weapon can broadly be classified as three: (i) their operational design implies the unjust conduct of war; (ii) the destruction they effect is on too great a scale; (iii) their methods are inhumane or cruel. Can these objections be validated by expressing them in terms of the traditional concerns over discriminate and proportionate conduct of hostilities? A working intuition might be that objections of type (i) correspond to concerns over discrimination, objections of type (ii) to concerns over proportion. This intuition needs exploration, as does the way in which objections of type (iii) may be accommodated within the traditional categories.

The term 'indiscriminate' is often applied to weapons of low precision or accuracy, or to weapons with uncontrollable side effects, but this is a misleading use of it. Discrimination has to do with the intention of attack, not with the technical limitations or grossness of the means. Can there, then, be such a thing as a weapon that is intrinsically indiscriminate? The paradigm case would be a biological weapon designed to spread dangerous viruses through the water supply. Its indiscriminacy would not depend upon its uncontrollable effects; it would be indiscriminate even if one could determine precisely the duration and diffusion of its effect. It would be indiscriminate because its mode of operation is to strike directly at the normal life-sustaining resources of a community, which are essentially common to military and civilian populations. If this weapon were used, it would make no sense to ask whether the destruction of the community's means of life was intended. It would be intended as a means to military victory, but intended none the less. It is not a matter of how many people are killed by it, or even how many civilians are killed compared with how many combatants. It is a matter of its structure of operation, which is an attack on a basic function of a community's life rather than on its military operations.

Alongside this paradigm case, let us put some others which differ from it in significant ways. The second example is also an imaginary weapon: a nuclear warhead in which the long-term radiation effects were deliberately enhanced – the precise opposite to the 'enhanced radiation' warhead or 'neutron bomb', which reduces long-term effect and enhances immediate effect in order to concentrate destructive power on the battlefield. This would be designed to make a virtue, presumably with deterrence in mind, of long-term social damage. To design such a weapon would be to intend especially the incremental long-lasting damage through cancer, food shortage, climatic instability and so on that would attach to any major nuclear explosion. As such we could only call such a weapon intrinsically indiscriminate. But it would not be so by virtue of its mode of operation as such, which would be the same as that of any other nuclear warhead, but by virtue of the special features which had been heightened. It would be indiscriminate only *in relation to* the original first-generation nuclear warhead of which it was a modification. Now consider, thirdly, a first-generation nuclear warhead, 'dirtier' in terms of long-term effects than the 'enhanced radiation' warheads which have been developed since. This, too, is indiscriminate in relation to an alternative; but here the alternative arose later, so that a weapon not originally susceptible to the judgment of indiscriminacy seems, paradoxically, to have become so simply by the accident of being superseded technologically. Anyone who deliberately maintains dirty weapons when clean ones are available is open to strong suspicion of indiscriminate intent; yet clearly this cannot be an *intrinsic* indiscriminacy in the weapon itself, which has not changed.

For a fourth example, let us consider the anti-personnel mine, the subject of a passionate campaign led by UNICEF, which culminated in the Ottawa Treaty of 1997, banning the sale and use of such weapons.[1] The feature that distinguishes mines from other weapons is that they are not deployed at the time of battle, but previously. Left hidden on the ground they hurt whoever runs into them, and so constitute a hazard to civilian populations and a bar to the economic development of valuable land in under-developed areas, as well as causing innumerable injuries of civilians, among whom children are especially vulnerable. Here, we may say, is a weapon which, while not incapable of discriminate use, is somewhat resistant to it. The traditional approach to regulation of these weapons assumed that a discriminate use was possible. The Second Protocol to the Inhumane Weapons Convention of 1981 defined and forbade indiscriminate use; it then imposed in general terms a régime of special precautions to protect civilians including mandatory mine-clearance, restricted the laying of hand-delivered mines to the vicinity of military objectives, and required protective signs, fences or guards to keep civilians away. Remotely delivered mines were restricted further: they might only be used in the vicinity of a military objective, and *either* an accurate record of their location may be kept *or* an effective self-neutralising device should be used. But this carefully thought-out approach came to seem inadequate, as the régime of discriminate use proved

---

[1] This came into effect on 1 March 1999, signed at the time by only 65 nations. Text at http://www.landmine.ro/legislat4.htm#Article%201, where 121 signatories were reported in January 2002 and 56 non-signatories, including, however, the USA, China, Russia, Pakistan, India and Israel.

virtually impossible to maintain. Apart from the fact that large numbers of belligerent forces, especially non-governmental ones, paid not the slightest heed to it, technological developments, replacing metal by plastic and reducing the size of the weapon, made the task of mine-clearance highly onerous and dangerous. Meanwhile, the promised development of an 'effective self-neutralising device' never reached a sufficient level of reliability. In this case, then, the charge of indiscriminacy against the weapon seems to be based on a political as well as a technological failure to develop and police what might have been an effective régime of discriminate use.

When we consider these four instances together, we see why the term 'indiscriminate' is extremely prone to slide from one meaning to another when applied to weapons. Its fundamental application is to the intention of an attack; but indiscriminate intention can affect weapons at a variety of stages: in design there may be indiscriminate intent, either in the mode of operation itself or in the choice of certain features to develop; in deployment there may be indiscriminate intent in the choice of one weapon over another, or in the failure to accept the disciplines that discriminate use of a weapon requires.

The logic of this extension of the word can be pressed further by way of a fifth application of the label 'indiscriminate', which is to any weapon of mass destruction. When a weapon can accomplish a certain scale of damage, it is argued, there is only one conceivable target for it, a city. And if we look not only at single explosions but at delivery systems which make it possible for such explosions to be multiplied, it is clear we are considering weapons intended to swallow whole metropolitan areas with all their inhabitants. It may seem a straightforward judgment that these systems propose indiscriminate slaughter, and are thus indiscriminate weapons. In which case we have justified the application of the term 'indiscriminate' simply on the grounds of scale alone.

The terms 'indiscriminate' and 'discriminate' are essentially qualifications of an *intention*. The possibility of speaking of indiscriminate weapons arises because indiscriminate intentions that lie behind their design or deployment are, for all practical purposes, manifest, either immediately or by inference. *Discriminate* intentions are not manifest in the same way, for there is no weapon that cannot be an instrument of indiscriminate intent, and that is why we find it less easy to speak of 'discriminate weapons', since there is no weapon on earth that could not be used indiscriminately. Design provides the most immediate evidence of indiscriminate intention. In our paradigm case, the biological weapon that is fed into the water supply, the attribution of indiscriminate intent depends only on our knowing that military and civilian water supplies cannot normally be kept separate. In this respect it is distinct from all the others. To reach the same judgment about the second example it is not enough to know how the weapon works; we need to know about its relation to alternative types of weapon. In the last three cases the judgment depends on an inference from a prior judgment that the collateral civilian damage involved in the weapon's use will necessarily be disproportionately large. The attribution of indiscriminate insane is obviously less secure in the third and fourth cases than in the fifth, since the range of possible reasons for failing to do what one might be expected to do is inevitably much greater than the range of possible reasons for doing what one might be expected not to do.

In these latter three cases, then, we attribute indiscriminacy only secondarily, having first made a judgment under the other major principle; so we must ask next whether there are any intrinsically disproportionate weapons. At first sight, this must appear an unpromising question, since proportion is, by its very nature, elastic. To say that we must not use means that are disproportionately destructive in relation to the threat we have to overcome is very well; but who knows what kind of threat we shall have to overcome? Not knowing in advance what history will bring forth, we do not know in advance what scale of resistance it may be proportionate to use.

However, this view is too sceptical. We can imagine a 'categorically disproportionate' mode of war, one which is out of proportion to any conceivable threat whatsoever. For although we do not know what threats the future will bring forth, we know what the conditions for human existence are, and we can imagine methods of defence that will defeat them. I gave as an example of a categorically disproportionate act of war the explosion of 6.33 megatons simultaneously in two hundred cities, an example I chose because it is believed to have been part of the range of NATO contingency plans developed in the cold-war period. I do not know whether there is a *single* weapon which, taken with its delivery system, would have consequences which are categorically incompatible with the pursuit of justice; so I cannot name a type of weapon, *each* example of which is categorically disproportionate, though there may well be one. We may be in doubt about this, and still be able to say that a nuclear stockpile *as a whole* is categorically disproportionate – making allowances, as one always must, for the fact that no power will intend to use all the armour in its armoury in one throw, but will keep different resources for different contingencies, and will plan to have something in reserve. A stockpile which allows contingency planning for the categorically disproportionate act in our example is likely to be a disproportionate stockpile.

There is, however, a second ground on which the principle of proportion might be used to prohibit types of weapon on the ground of scale: and that is that they have radically unpredictable consequences. We are, of course, only responsible for those consequences of our actions which we can foresee, and nobody may be blamed for everything that may follow from what he does. But when it is foreseeable that an act will launch the world on a train of unforeseeable consequences of untold peril, such an act must be disproportionate by the same principle that led Aristotle to say that we are responsible for what we do when we are drunk. If it is a moral principle that we should measure the scale of our destruction to the threat to ordered justice and peace, then that same principle forbids us knowingly to invoke unmeasurable destruction. It would seem that nobody is in a position to predict with any certainty what would follow from a single explosion of 6.33 megatons. Add to this the foreseeable likelihood, in a war in which both parties were equipped with nuclear weapons, of a retaliatory strike of corresponding severity; add the political unpredictability of such a situation in which it would be extremely hard to contain the belligerents from further nuclear exchange, and it would seem reasonable to conclude that here was a weapon which could never be used proportionately.

I do not know how far down the scale of magnitude a judgment of categorical disproportion would come. I am not inclined to think that *any* nuclear warhead, however small, would be included in it, despite the fact that any use of a nuclear weapon would create seriously unpredictable political consequences. Many smaller nuclear warheads may be probably, rather than categorically, disproportionate to use, only because of the risk of escalation and the powerful psychological threshold that separates nuclear from conventional weapons. But if all nuclear weapons other than the low-yield battlefield warheads had been effectively abolished, what remained might well take their place among the decent arsenals of civilised countries. However, it does seem certain that some nuclear warheads are categorically disproportionate, at least on the score of radically unpredictable consequences, and that whole nuclear arsenals, even those that remain today, are categorically disproportionate on the score of their certain destructiveness. And at this point we may repeat the inference we spelled out above: that if a weapon is categorically, and not just probably, disproportionate, then we may infer an indiscriminate intent as well.[2]

That is as far as we can go in the attempt to identify weapons of intrinsically immoral scale. But we ought to add that the morality of possessing weapons is not solely a matter of whether they are inherently immoral. Some weapons are inherently disproportionate to any conceivable political goal; others are probably disproportionate

---

[2] In *Peace and Certainty: A Theological Essay on Deterrence* (Oxford: Oxford University Press and Grand Rapids: Eerdmans, 1989) I addressed the question of whether the possession of weapons which it would be immoral to use could be justified for the purpose of deterrence.

to any likely political goal. The second of these judgments can be quite as significant for practical purposes. Action needs only to be based on a practical degree of certainty. To judge that certain weapons, or a certain quantity of weaponry, is gravely imprudent to possess, is not a light condemnation. Categorical prohibitions, though beloved of moral rhetoricians, are no more persuasive to the reasonable agent.

We have provided some modified support for the intuition that objections to operational design most closely relate to judgments of indiscriminacy, and that concerns over scale relate primarily to judgments of proportion. How are we to place objections to certain types of weapon as cruel or inhumane?

Any weapon may cause terrible and prolonged suffering. A conventional shell may kill three people outright and leave three more lingering in slow and painful death or facing a life of incapacitation. There is no point in criticising types of weapon for the suffering that may possibly be caused by them; that is part of the unavoidable horror of war. But there is scope for criticism where weapons cause suffering that could be avoided. It is a reasonable application of the principle of proportion that we should aim to minimise suffering produced by weapons by any means compatible with their effectiveness in battle. Consequently, the legal formula used in the 1981 Inhumane Weapons Convention prohibits 'superfluous injury or unnecessary suffering'.[3] That is to say, it condemns any gratuitous increment of suffering, whether for its own sake, for the sake of some strategic goal of deterrence, or as the result of carelessness. It need not be said, perhaps, that no increment of suffering would be 'gratuitous' or 'unnecessary' if it were implied in a genuine attempt to limit fatalities. It is sometimes objected to anti-personnel mines that they are not sufficiently destructive to kill, only to maim. If it is

---

[3] Adam Roberts and Richard Guelff, eds, *Documents on the Laws of War*, 2nd edn, Oxford, Oxford University Press, 1989, p. 473.

actually the case that some mines are calculated to inflict incapacitating injury, however dreadful, on victims who would *otherwise* be
killed, that can hardly be held as an objection to them. To reduce
fatalities in war is also a proper goal of proportionate conduct, and
indeed a prior goal to the reduction of suffering.

It is quite different, however, if weapons are designed to inflict injury first and *then* kill, *i.e.*, to inflict untreatable injuries. An example
of a cruel weapon of this description is found in the First Protocol
to the Convention, which prohibits 'any weapon the primary effect
of which is to injure by fragments which in the human body escape
detection by X-rays'.[4] This may count as a paradigm case of the cruel
weapon, which effects an increase of suffering for which there is no
military rationale. Serious casualties that would otherwise survive
become fatalities; but that hardly serves any military objective. The
only imaginable reason for using such weapons would be to spread
terror and despair.

Terror and despair can, no doubt, assist the accomplishment of
the military project; but they are not to be counted as either military
means or military ends. That an undertaking as hazardous and terrible as armed conflict will be accompanied by extreme psychological
states is obvious enough. But the military praxis is not a praxis of
manipulating psychological states; it is a praxis of denying the enemy
the freedom to act in certain ways. The discipline and legitimation
of military praxis depend on its self-containment within its proper
terms. 'Cruelty' arises precisely at the point where military praxis
spills over, as it were, into the pursuit of non-military goals, where
military means are deployed to solve non-military problems. The
term 'strategic' has often been employed to cover this expansion of
the military undertaking to embrace political goals. The *stratēgos* is a
general; but generals are dangerously amphibian creatures, half soldier, half politician, whose task it is to fit the military campaign into
the context of a political project. In so doing they must remember

[4] Ibid., p. 479.

the difference between undertakings that are properly political, not military, and what are properly military, not political. The manipulation of the enemy's moods, if it is a proper object of action at all, is not an object of military action, and must be done by politicians' speeches, not by weapons.

So much for the paradigm cruel weapon. What of weapons that for good operational reasons use means that involve acute suffering of some kind, such as the incendiary shells that attracted some public alarm during the Gulf War of 1991? The purpose of these is to get inside trenches, at which they are more effective than an explosive device. This weapon is not cruel in the sense we have described so far; but is there another sense in which it could be thought so? Does it, for instance, inflict a degree of suffering which ought not to be inflicted for any military necessity whatever? It is relevant in answering this question to notice that the fate which the incendiary shell inflicts, that of burning to death, is one that can quite easily be met on the battlefield by other means. It could be said, in fact, merely to extend a liability to this fate from artillery troops, for whom it is a constant danger, to infantry. Indeed, it is a fate not uncommonly encountered in civilian life, through aeroplane or motor accidents as well as through domestic fires, and although we take reasonable care to avoid it, we do not go to extreme lengths to do so.

This points us to an important question about the idea of a scale of suffering, to which we appeal when we speak of some weapons as causing 'more' suffering than they need, or 'excessive' suffering. What is this scale? Not, apparently, a scale of intensity of pain. Perhaps no more intense experience of pain can be imagined than that of burning to death, yet the incendiary weapon is not as obvious a candidate for the cruel weapon as the weapon which leaves undetectable fragments. The scale must also encompass such non-commensurable factors as duration of pain, hope of recovery from injury, and, the most difficult factor to describe but probably the deepest rooted, indignity and humiliation.

Consider, for example, a ruse which was said to have been practised during the Spanish Civil War: prostitutes who were medically
confirmed as carriers of venereal disease were infiltrated by Nationalist forces among Republican troops. If we can isolate what strikes
us as disgraceful about this measure, we may have a clue to the nature
of cruelty in weapons. There is, in the first place, the element of ruse
itself, and, in the second, the exploitation both of women as such and
of the tendency for male sexual self-discipline to break down under
pressure. Over and above these things there is something problematic
about the enterprise of deliberately communicating disease. Disease
attacks the bodily integrity of a person no more terribly than violent
assault; but because it attacks it from within, the deliberate communication of disease presents itself as a violation of personal autonomy
in a way that assault does not. We would not entertain for a moment
the idea that capital punishment might be administered that way,
let alone other punishments. All in all, we may say that this ruse
constituted an affront to human dignity.

And this is the best account I can come up with of why we have
felt it necessary to ban biological weapons as a class. Some of these
weapons, of course, are intrinsically indiscriminate and categorically
disproportionate, threatening grave and uncontrollable damage to
non-combatant populations. But there is no reason in principle why
we should not have 'battlefield' biological weapons that were 'clean'
of wider effects. Furthermore, the same criticisms can be made of
some nuclear weapons, and we have not banned those, let alone
all nuclear weapons as a class (though I think it contributes greatly
to public disquiet about nuclear weapons that they have carcino-
genic side effects). But the mode of operation of a biological weapon
puts it in a class apart, making it inhumane in a way that is independent of the mere scale of damage or intensity of suffering it
imposes.

If somebody finds this account of why we should keep biological weapons banned as a class inconclusive, I have two further

observations that I hope may at least make the opposite conclusion, that no distinction among classes of weapons is defensible, less attractive.

First, we would be wise to recognise the political value of conservative instincts in such matters, even if we cannot defend each instinctive judgment by independently sufficient reasons. There are, as I have suggested, some nuclear weapons that could properly take their place as part of a just arsenal; but that is not in itself a reason to resist the suggestion that the whole class of nuclear weapons should be banned. Someone who feels abhorrence for the class, though superficial, is not simply thoughtless. If the arguments I have advanced for a generic refusal of biological weapons are too weak, the refusal of them may still be right, simply because a prejudice towards caution in such matters is right. Such a prejudice may not justify everything it recommends, but can at least justify itself; its justification is that the search for new and ever more effective weapons technologies encourages cruelty of mind. The military ethos used to rely on courage and tactical imagination for its most important innovations, accepting technological advances as they arose, but without especially looking for them. The intense pursuit of military technology, however, must, as Mark Twain saw in his *Connecticut Yankee*, make the military enterprise less noble, breeding a race of inventors who do not have to contemplate at close quarters the harm that their inventions do.

My second observation is that, whether or not we can justify the prohibition of biological weapons on the grounds I have suggested, *some* lines of qualitative demarcation, not merely points on a quantitative scale, are relevant to defining cruelty. But disproportion is an essentially quantitative term, and so will not capture all that we mean and think when we say that a weapon is cruel or inhumane. If we are tough-minded we may wish to banish the notion of cruelty from the discussion altogether, but if we think it has any place, then we shall find ourselves trying to mark some qualitative thresholds, which will affect our thinking formally as a categorical prohibition, rather like the principle of discrimination. We shall recognise types of assault that are generically offensive to humanity, irrespective of how much damage they do or the suffering that they impose, types of assault which we should never adopt even for the sake of some weighty good to be achieved. These decisive determinants of human dignity will serve as a framework within which the military enterprise is confined *ab initio;* they will constitute categorical limits not subject to calculative negotiation.

In conclusion I make two fragmentary observations on how immoral weapons may be discouraged or controlled. The Ottawa Treaty abandoned the approach of the Second Protocol of the Inhumane Weapons Convention, which attempted to subject anti-personnel mines to a régime of discriminate use. It abandoned at the same time the hope which the Convention had placed in an 'effective self-neutralising device'. This may turn out to be a pity, since weak support for the Ottawa Treaty leaves it uncertain whether it will have any effect. It would be a bitter outcome indeed to all that campaigning if the net result of Ottawa was simply to discourage manufacturers from trying to perfect such a device. The risk that in trying to achieve more than is possible we may achieve a great deal less, is of constant importance to the discussion of war. Law is like a dyke built to contain the stream of human aspirations and ambitions: if we want to contain the floodwaters, we must leave a channel just large enough for them to find their way to the sea.

The Ottawa Treaty raised by implication two difficult questions: (a) whether supply-side control of weapons is possible; (b) whether a generic prohibition can be made sufficiently specific from a technical point of view to exclude the weapons most properly objected to.

(a) Each party undertook not only not to use, but not to 'develop, produce, otherwise acquire, stockpile, retain *or transfer*' such weapons. Hitherto, most international law controlling weapons has been directed at *use*, though it has sometimes gone so far as to prohibit testing. A great deal of public enthusiasm has been shown for the argument for strong supply-side control, even for the total dismantling of the market in armaments. The Nuclear Non-proliferation Treaty has illustrated the dangers that an unreflective rush to transfer prohibition might create. A series of nations with strong fighting traditions in regions of the world where tension is endemic have attempted to acquire the capacity for independent production of nuclear weapons under cover of national state secrecy. International monitoring has been extremely difficult, even with such comparatively traceable materials as are needed for nuclear weapons, and the political difficulties of confronting offenders have themselves sometimes brought war dangerously close, as in the case of North Korea. Imagine reproducing this situation for conventional arms with legitimate uses, and on a worldwide basis! Other considerations apart, the economic strain on developing countries, forced to mount a domestic arms industry because they could not purchase what they needed, would be cataclysmic.

Measures controlling commercial operations need to encourage independent commercial responsibility. Swingeing prohibitions create black markets; well-drafted regulations create responsible markets, in which there are major dealers who have an interest in seeing that the rules are kept. Those who make and sell arms must be allowed the opportunity to make and sell *acceptable* arms. What are the features we should look for in a responsible market? In the first place, publicity. The creation of the Conventional Arms Transfer Register in 1992 was an important step towards allowing the world to know who was buying what and from whom. In the second place, we should expect a refusal to deal with illegitimate purchasers, such as non-governmental actors, who should not, as a rule, be able to procure heavy arms. Thirdly, we should expect tight credit control, so that excessive purchases are not made on lax credit or soft currency. Here the existence of a commercial market that functions independently of government may be a positive advantage, since governments have shown more than a little tendency to allow arms transfers to become disastrously entangled with forms of inter-governmental co-operation and exchange, such as humanitarian or development aid.

There is good reason to doubt that arms-transfer control from the supply side can be wholly effective. Whether it can be effective *enough* depends on such a ban being accompanied by credible measures against use. That is to say, the provisions of the Ottawa Treaty also need the effective operation of the Protocol to the Inhumane Weapons Convention to make any impact on landmines at all. Supply control may, however, make a serious contribution to solving the problem of landmines, *if* the second question is satisfactorily answered.

A ban has to be directed against certain *specific technical features* of a weapon. It may seem a simple matter to name a class of weapon for prohibition, but weapons technology is fluid. In ruling something out, a ban presents an incentive to technology to overcome the new handicap it has imposed. Careless specification of precisely what is objected to will result in the same, or some more objectionable, feature coming back in a new form on a new generation of weapons with new names. The Ottawa Treaty defines an anti-personnel mine as one 'exploded by the presence, proximity or contact of a person'; but excludes anti-vehicle mines equipped with an anti-handling device, which 'activates when an attempt is made to . . . disturb the mine'. One does not have to be too pessimistic to fear a new generation of anti-handling devices which will make anti-vehicle mines an effective substitute for the banned anti-personnel mine. It is essential that prohibitions are so framed as to direct the efforts of weapons technologists in the right direction, as the Inhumane Weapons Convention attempted to do in allowing a self-neutralising device, in the hope that one would soon be perfected.

Weapons technology has terrorised the twentieth century by running ahead of moral, political and legal control. It is easy to deplore its past rôle; but the practical question is always how to bring it under control. We are still a technology-led society and events will continue to unfold in the way they have done, unless we make it our business to set our weapons designers to work upon specific tasks which will comprise, as it were, a discipline of penance. Prohibitions are unhelpful, unless accompanied by a serious attempt to apply moral reasoning to the task of weapons design.

4 | War by other means

In the introduction to his major work, *On War*, Carl von Clausewitz wrote his most quoted dictum: 'War is nothing but the continuation of policy with other means.'[1] What he meant by this, as he explained in his eighth book, was that war was not an intelligible enterprise apart from political reason. It had to be an 'instrument' of policy, and instruments always derive their intelligibility from the ends they serve. Read in this sense the dictum is the purest practical wisdom, and certainly supports the disciplining of war by morality. However, it has consistently been read as a slightly cynical observation; and that, I take it, is because Clausewitz relates war to 'policy' rather than to international justice. This tends to suggest that warfare between sovereign states is an uncomplicated and unambiguous exposition of the ordinary purposes of the state. The appearance of purely self-interested national communities exercising their strength upon their neighbours' defences is a true disclosure of the character of the civil community. This hint Clausewitz develops in a somewhat romantic nineteenth-century direction, adding his voice to the view that vitality and will are the truest realities, and that if war is the authentic prophet of national will, total war is the most outspoken form of authentic prophecy.

'War by other means': This essay was first published in Roger Williamson, ed., *Some Corner of a Foreign Field: Intervention and World Order*, Basingstoke, Macmillan, 1998, pp. 87–98. I am grateful for the agreement of the publisher to its being reproduced here.

[1] Carl von Clausewitz, *On War*, ed. and trans. M. Howard and P. Paret, London, Everyman's Library, 1993, p. 77.

I want to reverse the order of the dictum and speak, instead, of the various ways in which we may continue *war* 'by other means'. For if Clausewitz thought that war discloses the true nature of state policy, then, I suggest, we should say that he got it exactly the wrong way round. The normal activities of the state disclose the true nature of war, and teach us to see it as an act of judgment, serving the need of the international community for just order. This reconstruction of the idea of war happens in two stages. The first is the disciplining of the resort to war and the means of war, bringing them under the threefold constraint of authority, proportion and discrimination. The second is the devising of intermediate means, which stand between serious political conflict and the outbreak of war, and provide a range of responses which will perhaps avert the necessity of resort to armed conflict.

We begin, then, with the idea of war as a pure expression of state policy, and of total war as its most complete expression, and we learn to conceive of just war as force put under the discipline, and in the service, of justice. But then we move from just war to 'war by other means', which is to say a flexible range of intermediate measures, which depend on the marginal possibility of resort to war but serve to keep it at arm's length. This second stage is similar to the task of scaling down the language of punishment, so that we are not forced constantly to resort to the execution of criminals. And in each case we must say that we cannot devise intermediate means if we fail to understand what the extreme means were intended to accomplish. The search for intermediate alternatives to war must come *after* the decision that our wars should be just. If we begin from a posture of simple opposition to war, we will lose sight of this logical order by thrusting the search for 'some other way' to the fore. But 'some other way' to do what? Not just to 'discuss our differences', but to resolve issues of right justly and effectively. Intermediate means that are not designed to do this are not intermediate means at all. They are simply an excuse for avoiding the task of international justice.

What are the true 'intermediate alternatives' that stand between parties in conflict and outright war? First, there is the symbolic language of diplomacy, which expresses judgment by such means as expelling diplomats, severing relations, lodging protests and so on. This language makes no direct appeal to power; but its effect is entirely derived from the fact of power and from the possibility, which lies on the horizon, of deploying force. Such gestures act as warning indicators, and are an excellent example of how the ultimate possibility of force supports a proximate language which can proceed at a distance from force.

Diplomacy continues war by other means; but those other means are not acts of war. There are other kinds of alternative means which are, formally considered, acts of war, in that they involve the actual exercise of power beyond the sphere of political authority; and yet they are alternatives to what we conventionally understand as acts of war. In the first place, there are uses of force that are designed to overcome opposition without directly intending fatalities. The deployment of tear gas, or of other incapacitating gases, is an example of this. In the second place, there are uses of power which are not uses of force. It is on the most controversial of these that I wish to concentrate: economic sanctions.

First of all, we must distinguish economic sanctions, as used by one hostile state or group of states against another, from other and similar-looking gestures, which are, however, in a different moral category and do not constitute acts of war.

(i) Sanctions are distinct from a *selective refusal to trade* with, or invest in, immoral businesses or sectors of business. Imagine a nation that makes a considerable export market out of addictive drugs; and consider the status of laws in other nations forbidding the import of, and banning trade in, those drugs. It would be wrong to construe those laws as a hostile act towards the exporting nation. The decision not to permit trade in such goods is intelligible solely on its own terms, and is logically independent of any decision about how to deal with nations that encourage the trade. It is a question of refusal to trade with immoral businesses. And the business may be immoral either because the goods it deals in are immoral or because those who run the business have no moral standing to do so. The trade in slaves may be prohibited because slaves ought not to be bought or sold; the trade in artefacts made by slaves may be prohibited because the vendors have no proper title to the property in which they deal. For similar reasons we ban a trade in ivory which depends heavily on the work of poachers and is, as such, environmentally destructive – even though, as some African countries remind us, it is possible to run a responsible trade in ivory which is actually beneficial environmentally. None of these prohibitions are acts of war, even though whole nations may be damagingly affected by them.

In principle they are not discretionary. Once the character of the improper business has become clear, there is a moral obligation not to trade with it, because one is required not to co-operate in wrong. It is, of course, *politically* discretionary for a government to *criminalise* such trading, as there always is an element of political discretion about the implementation of moral principle in criminal law. But individual business-people who understand the nature of the enterprises and continue to trade with them are acting wrongly. What applies to trading applies *a fortiori* to investment. Trading is minimally co-operative; and we usually say that the purchaser of goods bears only a small responsibility to establish the bona fides of goods offered for sale in the market-place – yet even so, that small burden of responsibility may require the boycott of scandalous goods. A greater burden of responsibility rests on those who invest, since investment is positively co-operative. One of the great disadvantages of arm's length dealing in the stock market is that neither the investor nor the financial corporation who sells the unit trusts may assume responsibility for enquiring into the morality of the businesses concerned.

What is in question in the selective refusal to trade is the nature of the business itself, not the nature of the society or the state which supports it. In the term 'business', of course, we may include a whole sector of business in a given country, where conditions are inhuman or pay inadequate. But such a judgment is always relative to what is reasonably possible within that society. To know that workers on coffee plantations only take home so much a year, tells us nothing. We need to know what could be done, given good will, within the constraints of the market and the social setting; and only then do we know whether we are looking at an immoral sector of business. Any measures of this first kind, whether legislated or voluntary, are directed against types of business practice. Legislation implementing them must be framed generically, specifying the kinds of enterprise involved. If, instead of such legislation, government were to act executively, naming the countries or companies involved, it would cross the line that separates selective refusal to trade from sanctions, and would commit itself to an act of war.

(ii) Different from this first policy, and still distinct from sanctions, is the policy of *dissociation* from societies which tolerate or encourage behaviour unacceptable to the international community. Under this heading is included the severing of wider cultural as well as business contacts, and this is done on a non-selective basis, irrespective, that is, of whether the activities in question are conducted immorally. We have, in the past, refused sports contacts even with racially integrated sports associations in apartheid South Africa. The point of these measures is penal, but they fall short of an exercise of power, and so do not constitute a penal act of war. They aim to communicate to the society in question the disapproval in which it is held; and they are chosen for their symbolic and expressive power, rather than for any special guilt incurred within the activities suspended, and – more importantly – rather than for any leverage they may have upon the policies of that state. The penalty is informal. It operates at the sub-political level, and for that reason may often be conceived as part of an ongoing remonstrance with that society in which dissociation at one level (say, culture) is offset by intensified communication at another (say, between religious leaders). In invoking such measures the future of the conversation, and the possibility of its actually having a beneficial effect, have to be borne in mind.

This is a conversation between societies rather than governments. It is important that societies should be able to communicate informal judgments on each other in a manner that does not require the use of state power. This protects society's moral reflection on international affairs from the constraints of *Realpolitik* which inevitably affect a state. A society which cannot form, and express, judgments on its neighbours except when its government tells it to, is not a free society. For that reason I confess I saw much good sense in the rather unpopular policy of the British government for many years, of encouraging, but not requiring, cultural gestures of dissociation from apartheid South Africa. Once government starts requiring hostile acts against another state, then a threshold of some importance has been crossed; and once it is crossed, the basis for selecting the measures must change. Then its aim must be to impose judgment upon the recalcitrant offender, and its measures must be chosen precisely for their effectiveness in doing that. At that point we cross into sanctions.

(iii) Different again, and still distinct from sanctions, are what international lawyers call *acts of retorsion*. These are acts performed by states, which, though they are intended to be hostile, lie perfectly within the state's sphere of political authority and would not constitute an offence, whatever the circumstances in which they were performed. Examples might be: cutting off aid, refusing preferential access to domestic markets, banning arms sales. All these things lie within the jurisdiction of the state. It does not lie within the jurisdiction of a state to prevent another state's growing rich, developing its trading, or arming itself; but it does lie within its discretion in the conduct of its own foreign policy to discourage these developments; and if a state is to carry through its foreign policy effectively, it must be able to command support from its citizens, including those who give aid, trade, or sell armaments.

Not all trade falls directly within the scope of a state's foreign policy; but the making of special treaties offering trading privileges does; and so does trade in arms, or in any other goods which may be instruments of hostility or oppression. Computer programs, for example, suitable for a police force needing to keep extensive records of dissidents, might be included in a trade ban with respect to a particular country in which the government judged that there was a police state. This ban is not, as such, an act of war, but an act of policy. (This is still the case when a number of states agree a common policy on banning arms' sales.) If, however, the government undertook active measures to prevent the disfavoured state from importing arms from other countries which would otherwise be willing to export them, then it would become more than an act of retorsion and would have to be classified as a 'reprisal', which belongs within the category of 'sanction' as I am using the term.

Sanctions are acts of war which do not involve the direct use of force. They employ the power of the state, or more probably of a number of allied states, in a way that would constitute an offence against the opposing state were it not for that state's prior offence which has given just cause for war. Sanctions are thus 'reprisal' rather than 'retorsion'. But I include general trade embargoes in the category of sanctions in defiance of the consensus of international lawyers, who maintain that these cannot be reprisals because they would not be illegal otherwise. The moralist is in a happy position with regard to legal categories; he can plunder them at will, and revise them as he chooses, to purge them from the taint of sin! In this case I argue that everyone has a basic right of access to commerce with everyone else, subject only to such regulatory control as is necessary to protect the common good, and that a general ban on trade with a given country, even if not illegal in law, is overtly hostile and ought to be considered as an offence, unless it is justified as an act of war.

The decision to impose sanctions is already a decision to make war. If we fail to acknowledge this, we will fail to ask the relevant questions about the justice of the sanctions, and these two questions in particular: (1) whether in the particular circumstances sanctions can be imposed in a way conformable to the restraints of just war; (2) whether in the particular circumstances sanctions are more appropriate than other modes of hostility. Let us take first the question of conformability to just-war restraints. Can sanctions be discriminate? And can they be proportionate?

It is clear that sanctions can be indiscriminate, and that *general* economic sanctions are always likely to be indiscriminate. They strike directly at the ordinary, life-sustaining functions of the community. When used with great effect, they result in famine, the first victims of which are the poor and other vulnerable sectors of society – the sick, the old and children. We may be tempted to think them categorically immoral, for the same reason that biological warfare directed at the water supply is immoral. They attack the life of society as such, not the threat posed by the activities of the state to other societies. It is important here to understand the structural difference between economic sanctions and the traditional siege. A siege used to be undertaken in order to inhibit troops from free movement. Civilians in a besieged city might starve; but that was not the point of the operation, and you would always prefer, other things being equal, to pin your enemy's forces down in a city which had been deserted by its civilian inhabitants. General economic sanctions, however, aim to affect the political will of the hostile government through the economic straits into which the population at large is thrown. If the population is unaffected, the whole strategy has failed, since there was no other way in which they were going to persuade the government to change its mind. This is bad enough; but when the sanctions are directed against a government to persuade it to stop mistreating a part of its own population, as in the cases of Rhodesia and South Africa, there is the additionally distressing consideration that the first to suffer will quite probably be the very population it was intended to defend. We ought to notice that the argument which used to be held in support of general sanctions against South Africa – that if the black leadership was in favour of sanctions, it was not for us to be over-scrupulous about them – is without any force. We were answerable for the methods by which we chose to make war; and the black community was not entitled to offer us its children and elderly to use as weapons against the white government.

Into this unpromising picture, however, we can introduce a factor which allows some flexibility. Sanctions can be varied in their severity and in focus. Directed against investment, they may attack the capital on which the industrial organisation of a complex economy rests, and so destroy the society's prosperity, but not its capacity to sustain a subsistence. Given certain types of economy, with a developed industrial sector on top of a capacity for food production that is essentially self-sufficient, general economic sanctions will not produce famine, though they may produce grave social disruption. And where the food production is not self-sufficient, the sanctions may be tailored to allow subsistence imports while still maintaining a stranglehold on capital and industrial resources. This is what the UN tried to achieve in the 'smart' sanctions on Iraq. If general economic sanctions are deployed in this way, directly attacking capital and industry but not subsistence, may our negative judgment be mitigated, even though they are still formally 'indiscriminate'?

The classic just-war theorists drew a sharp distinction between the claim of the innocent on their lives and their claim on their property. Suárez, in a judgment that may strike us as cold-blooded, says: '[I]t is permitted to deprive the innocent of their goods, even of their liberty, if such a course of action is essential to complete satisfaction. The reason is that the innocent form a portion of one whole and unjust state.'[2] However, 'innocent persons, as such, may absolutely not be killed'. This, he argues, is because:

[2] Suárez, *De triplici virtute theologica*, 3.13.7, in Oliver O'Donovan and Joan Lockwood O'Donovan, eds, *From Irenaeus to Grotius*, Grand Rapids, Eerdmans, 1999, p. 740.

Life is not the same as other possessions. They fall under human dominion, and the state as a whole has a higher right over them than particular persons; so they may be deprived of their property for the guilt of the whole. But life does not fall under human dominion, so that no one may be deprived of life other than for his own guilt.[3]

When we have recovered from the shock of his permission for taking slaves as reparations (though only of non-Christians, and even heretics are not to be included!), we may perhaps see some good moral sense in Suárez's refusal to extend to the property of non-combatants that immunity from direct attack that he extends to their lives. The argument that wealth 'falls under human dominion' may be paraphrased like this: the power to accumulate wealth depends on the state's protection of an advanced social organisation; property owners are such by virtue of the conditions the state has maintained, and to that degree their property is not inalienably their own in the sense that their lives are. This argument may be compared with one that is sometimes heard, that the wealthy are *ipso facto* complicit in the oppression of the poor. This stronger argument seems to me to be badly overstated but to have a grain of truth in it. Wealth as such is not a form of aggression; and if it were, then the wealthy would, as such, be combatants, their lives and not merely their property forfeit. But wealth may sometimes depend on aggression, even on an aggression that is not that of its owners; or it may depend on political conditions which have permitted aggression to take place unchecked; and for these reasons it cannot be viewed, as it is in the Lockean tradition, as a kind of extension of the person, enjoying the same immunities that the person enjoys.

We may note in passing that Suárez's argument applied in favour of targeted sanctions on capital and industry does not depend upon the 'principle of double effect', *i.e.*, the distinction between directly voluntary and indirectly voluntary harm. If the property of non-combatants is as such a legitimate object of attack, there is no question

---

[3] Ibid., p. 741.

of such an attack being 'indiscriminate'. The principle of double effect does not apply. That is because it is not, as has often been claimed, a general formal rule governing all cases of ambiguity in moral choice. It is a rule that applies only, or primarily, to the taking of innocent life, and cannot confidently be extrapolated beyond this sphere.[4]

Moving on to the second question, it is clear that general economic sanctions can be disproportionate. They take longer than military action to have effect, and they expose societies to various consequential ills with long-term implications, including the breakdown of civil order. The experience of Britain in imposing sanctions, in co-operation with the UN, on the rebel régime in Rhodesia in 1965 is illuminating. When the rebellion occurred, the government of the day resorted to sanctions because it was not confident of popular support for a cumbersome military operation in Central Africa against colonial settlers with whom there was a strong feeling of kinship. Extravagant hopes were entertained of the speed with which sanctions would 'bring the rebel régime to its knees' – 'weeks rather than months' was one unfortunate prediction. In fact it took ten years, and part of the cost was the slow collapse of Rhodesia-Zimbabwe into a civil war conducted by guerrilla methods which inflicted extensive suffering on innocent victims both white and black. The 'success' of sanctions in this case was somewhat Pyrrhic, and suggests strongly that an initial military endeavour, however difficult to mount, might have been more prudent. Certainly it would have given the new state of Zimbabwe a better start in life. I assume in this argument that not a single death was *directly* attributable to sanctions (which would be an argument for them as indiscriminate). The deaths caused *indirectly* over the space of ten years constitute the argument for disproportion, if they outweighed the likely cost of an immediate military operation.

It is clear from this that the decision to impose sanctions presupposes a conviction that they are the appropriate means of war

---

[4] Cf. my *Resurrection and Moral Order*, Leicester, Apollos, 2nd edn, 1994, pp. 192–3.

for the circumstances. Much of the problem surrounding Western sanctions against apartheid South Africa sprang from the idea that sanctions were an *alternative* to war, rather than an alternative *mode* of war. Western powers, though they might have offered military aid to the front-line states if they had become involved in a South African civil war, were not ready to contemplate direct military involvement themselves. This meant that the question was not put in the form that it should have been: whether sanctions were the appropriate means for performing an act of judgment against the South African régime.

It is arguable that, in fact, they were the appropriate means. Sanctions commend themselves as a means of intervention into a domestic struggle, in which the international community has a comparatively weak *locus standi* in international law. Wars of intervention are not ruled out legally, if conducted under UN authorisation, by the UN Charter. The Security Council is entitled to concern itself with any 'dispute, the continuation of which is likely to endanger the maintenance of international peace and security', which includes internal disputes within states when they are of such an order as to draw other states into conflict with them.[5] Morally, too, we may say that there should be no outright bar against a war of intervention, given sufficient cause. Nevertheless, there is a strong presumption against wars of intervention, based on respect for the authority of each state to govern its people; and this presumption is appropriately acknowledged by a preference for hostilities which do not involve armed intrusion on to the hostile state's territory.

Intervention into a state's internal conflicts, then, is one type of conflict for which sanctions appear especially appropriate. Another is when military operations face severe logistical impediments – though perhaps this is the most treacherous type. A third is to provide a first,

---

[5] Charter of the United Nations, 33, in Ian Brownlie, ed., *Basic Documents in International Law*, Oxford, Oxford University Press, 5th edn, 2002, p. 10.

mild stage in the hostilities, to bring moderate pressure to bear to achieve a settlement, if possible, before the resort to arms becomes necessary. This was the use to which sanctions were appropriately put prior to the Gulf conflict in 1991. But that case illuminates two general principles very clearly. In the first place, economic sanctions raise fewest problems when directed against a developed industrial economy which is adequately self-sufficient in food production to maintain its subsistence. By the time that military operations began in January 1991 it was claimed by Iraq that 4,000 people from vulnerable sectors of the population had in the course of six months died of conditions related to undernourishment; and although this information came from a tainted source, independent observers of the flow of rural refugees leaving Iraq for Jordan thought it not improbable. Sanctions were, as was claimed at the time, 'working' – but working in precisely the way one does not want them to work, undermining subsistence rather than capital. In the second place, then, the Gulf experience demonstrated the necessity of having clearly in mind what was to be done if sanctions failed to achieve the purpose within tolerable limits of damage to the community. A decision needed to be made at the point of imposing sanctions what the next step would be – whether to abandon the attempt altogether, or to go forward to military activity.

And here we see why it is treacherous to impose sanctions in situations where military action faces insuperable obstacles. If there is no further stage to the hostilities that can be envisaged, the temptation will be to maintain the sanctions indefinitely, even when they can be seen to be inflicting indiscriminate destruction on the population, as subsequent events in Iraq have illustrated. The temptation will be even worse if it has never been admitted that sanctions are an act of war, and they are interpreted, in bad faith, merely as a kind of 'statement' of disapproval. A belligerent has a duty to bring the warfare to a decisive conclusion. A besieging army may have to attempt to storm the garrison in order to end the privation and misery within it, even if it would suit its own purposes much better just to sit there until there was no one left alive. Similarly, those who impose sanctions have to have an exit strategy, and must reckon with the possibility that other action may be needed to bring their economic siege to an end. The appeal of sanctions to a civilisation that loves strong moral statements but hates war is a seductive one, but possibly fatal.

5 | Can war crimes trials be morally satisfying?

The classic just-war theorists of the sixteenth century assumed that the conclusion of hostilities would, as a matter of course, be marked by an attempt on the part of the victors to punish the vanquished, by confiscations, executions, and possibly the deposition of the ruler. They never questioned the right to such exercises of *post bellum* jurisdiction, but they inclined to discourage them and to limit their scope. Their reasons can be summarised as three.

(a) It encouraged, they feared, the vices of implacability and vengefulness, attitudes inconsistent with the judicial frame of mind fundamental to a just war. 'It is necessary to preserve in war the same equality as in a just judgment,' wrote Suárez. Vitoria, in the fine peroration of his lecture on the Law of War, invited the victor to 'think of himself as a judge sitting in judgment between two commonwealths, the one the injured party and the other the offender; he must not pass sentence as the prosecutor but as a judge'. The conduct of the victor, then, must be discriminating, making a point of distinguishing those especially active in promoting the unjustified hostilities from the innocent. 'It does not suffice', wrote Grotius, 'that we conceive the enemy, by some fiction, as though they were a single body.'[1]

'Can War crimes trials be morally satisfying?': I am grateful to R. John Pritchard for his agreement to my publishing for the first time here this essay, commissioned for an extensive series of volumes, *The British Trials of Japanese War Criminals 1946–8*, still forthcoming. I am grateful also to Professor Adam Roberts, who commented on a draft, and to the Rev. Dr. Shinji Kayama, of Rokkakubashi Church, Yokohama, who supplied me with material on the Tokyo trials.

[1] Francisco Suárez, *De triplici virtute theologica* 3.13.7.7, in *Selections from Three Works*, ed. J.B. Scott, Classics of International Law, Oxford, Clarendon Press, 1944, vol. II,

(b) They feared, too, a strict-liability criterion, which would fail to distinguish the true *mens rea* not only from the sheer misfortune of being caught up in hostilities but also from what Grotius called an 'intermediate fault', which, though it should be liable to damages, ought not to incur punishment. There could be good faith in a bad cause. This consideration ought probably to excuse subordinates as a matter of course, for 'subjects usually fight in good faith for their princes' (Vitoria). Yet princes, too, could pursue bad causes in good faith: 'there are causes which, without being actually just, can seem impressive to those who are not bad men' (Grotius). Two factors, then, enter into this 'good faith'. One is an epistemological variable in moral and political judgment: a point of view may make a bad cause seem good. The other is the context of political loyalties, indispensable to the existence of any political society. Subjects owe their rulers the benefit of the doubt, and if the benefit may sometimes prove to have been undeserved, that does not mean they were wrong to give it.[2]

(c) They saw the danger that judicial zeal might provide further fuel for conflict. New causes of war could be added to old. Grotius, whose theory was distinctive, explained some of the more common licences of war as *indemnities from prosecution*, conferred by customary international law upon acts which common morality (the 'Law of Nature') would forbid. The reason for these indemnities he explained as follows: questions of *ius ad bellum* could hardly be determined by any third party without the danger of its being drawn into the hostilities; questions of *ius in bello* were, in any case, virtually impossible for anyone to settle with objectivity, so that only in the forum of the conscience could they be resolved at all. This theory, though original, summed up the practice which other thinkers of the age expected

---

p. 841. Francisco di Vitoria, *De iure belli relectio*, concl. In *Vitoria: Political Writings*, ed. Anthony Pagden & Jeremy Lawrance, Cambridge, Cambridge University Press, 1991, p. 237. Hugo Grotius, *De iure belli ac pacis* 3.11.16., ed. B.J.A. de Kanter-van Hettinga Tromp, R. Feenstra and C.E. Persenaire, Aalen, Germany, Scientia Verlag, 1993, p. 759.

[2] Grotius, 3.11.4, p. 741; 3.11.6, p. 747. Vitoria, *De iure*, in *Political Writings*, p. 237.

and recommended: *ius ad bellum* offences were to be punished, but selectively, by the victors; *ius in bello* offences were to be punished by nobody. Remarkably, this generation of theorists, which achieved so sharp a focus on the principles governing the conduct of war, never seriously doubted that they were unjusticiable.[3]

But in subsequent generations a seismic shift in the theoretical bedrock produced a turn of thought which put an end to the idea of *post bellum* justice. The concept of a unitary Natural Law was steadily fragmented into a plurality of natural rights, and the concept of war as an informal procedure of *justice* gave way to that which saw it as an unarbitrable contest of *interests*. Grotius's *obiter dictum* about the difficulties of third-party involvement was used as the basis of a new, more sceptical theory (a fate which befell some others of his observations at the hands of later admirers): in voluntary international law, claimed Vattel, 'regular war, as to its effects, is to be accounted just on both sides'. From this it was not a large step to concluding that no one, not even the victor, could pretend to exercise jurisdiction over the crime of making unjust war. Kant drew the inference uncompromisingly: 'The victor lays down the conditions on which it will come to an agreement with the vanquished and hold *negotiations* for concluding peace. The victor does not do this from any right he pretends to have because of the wrong his opponent is supposed to have done him; instead, he lets this question drop and relies on his own force.' With this the collapse of the just-war idea was complete. For Kant's idealist pacifism the only rationally just thing to be done in war was, by any means not excluding conquest, to put an end to it.[4]

But moral sentiment, like volcanic lava, will erupt somewhere. By the latter half of the nineteenth century the self-consciously amoral account of war, for which Kant was the philosophical spokesman, was being overtaken by a new search for judicial and moral principles,

---

[3] Grotius, 3.4.4, p. 659.

[4] Emmerich de Vattel, *The Law of Nations* 3.190. Trans. J. Chitty, Philadelphia, Johnson, 1863, p. 382. Emmanuel Kant, *The Metaphysics of Morals*, The Doctrine of Right, 58. Trans. Mary Gregor, Cambridge, Cambridge University Press, 1991, p. 154.

a search that bore fruit in the Geneva Convention of 1864 and the Hague Conventions of 1889 and 1907. But now it was *ius in bello* principles that were especially in view; and that has been generally the case throughout the great twentieth-century enterprise of codifying the law of war and making it justiciable. Although the Nuremberg Charter authorised the prosecution of 'crimes against peace', war crimes were the primary concern of that tribunal and of others, just as they were of the major conventions, of the Hague and of Geneva, which marked the progress of the enterprise.[5] An unsteady progress it has been. The invention of the military aeroplane so soon after the Hague Conventions came into effect produced a dangerous aneurysm in the provisions to protect civilians from attack, leaving the so-called 'humanitarian law' – the body of law concerned with the wounded, the sick and prisoners – to carry the weight of the enterprise throughout the middle of the century, until the situation was repaired by the First Geneva Protocol in 1977.[6]

But can legal provisions do more than simply fashion expectations? Do conventions and codified law permit us to reverse the presumption of unjusticiability? The actual experience of War Crimes Tribunals in the wake of the Second World War takes us a certain distance towards a positive answer. Yet they did not remove the three causes of anxiety which concerned the classic just-war thinkers.

(a) Although there was a serious attempt to place the Nuremberg and Tokyo Tribunals on an international footing, nothing can hide the fact that they were convened at the initiative of the victorious

---

[5] Judgment of the International Military Tribunal at Nuremberg. In Adam Roberts and Richard Guelff, eds, *Documents on the Law of War*, 2nd edn, Oxford, Oxford University Press, 1989, pp. 153–6, together with Prefatory Note. Crimes against peace played a major part in the indictment against the principal defendants in the Tokyo trials.

[6] Ibid., pp. 387–446. The provisions of this treaty, though not formally binding since Iraq was not a signatory, certainly shaped the strategy of the alliance forces in the Gulf War of 1991, which thus became the first important test of the practicability of its provisions. On the significance of strategic air war in twentieth-century military doctrine see Lawrence Freedman, *The Evolution of Nuclear Strategy*, London, Macmillan, 1981, pp. 4–14.

allies, 'for the just and prompt trial and punishment of the major war criminals of the European Axis', on one side only, that is, of the conflict just concluded.[7] No doubt the military discipline was in general much better on the other side. Still, it is notoriously difficult for any belligerent party to take a judicious view of war crimes committed in its own service – as the 1970 trial of William Calley for the My-Lai massacre and his subsequent pardon indicate all too clearly. And there was no forum in which the allies' interpretation of international law – notoriously lenient on the question of strategic bombing of cities – could be challenged. The work of those tribunals, however scrupulous in itself, is overshadowed by the philosophy of *Vae victis!* which seems to have engendered them.

(b) The Nuremberg principle of 'individual responsibility' to the laws of war, whereby the orders of a superior would count in mitigation only and not in defence, deliberately turns its back upon the generous presumption of 'good faith' which the classic theorists were anxious to maintain. Of course, the presumption of good faith is rebuttable; and many of the offences were so dreadful as to afford a satisfactory rebuttal. Still, it leaves behind a disturbing legacy of legal doctrine, some of the implications of which became evident in the trials of former East Berlin border guards. Actions arising in a political or legal context gravely deficient in justice cannot be assessed 'in themselves', as though the context were not there. This is to bring an abstract moralism – no less abstract and no less moralistic if it is armed with texts of international law – to take the place of careful attention to the act, considered concretely in all its aspects and within its own context. Such moralism is bad morality – and it can do international law no good to be tied to doctrines which offend moral sensibilities.

(c) The success of the political reconstruction of West Germany and Japan removed any fear that further conflict might be generated

---

[7] Constitution of the International Military Tribunal, August 1945. Text at http://elsinore.cis.yale.edu/lawweb/avalon/imt/proc/imtconst.htm.

by the judicial exercise. Still, we should not ignore the implications of the fact that those trials were conducted under conditions of occupation, in which the normal responsibilities of government could be selectively assumed by the occupying powers. Such circumstances do not always arise at the conclusion of hostilities. Nor should we hope that they will. It would be a disaster if the institutions of *post bellum* justice created a political pressure to fight wars *à l'outrance* and to refuse moderate settlements in which each government remained intact. The Gulf War of 1991 invited us to reflect on what might have been involved had the alliance been committed to bringing the Iraq leadership to trial, for which, after all, there was an exceptionally good *prima facie* case. Furthermore, the experience of counter-guerrilla and counter-terrorist operations teaches us how trials for terrorism may simply stoke up conflict.

Yet there are good reasons for not abandoning the idea of trying war crimes. Though law may have an influence simply by creating expectations, it cannot do that very effectively for very long without the help of court judgments to reinforce it. *Lex scripta*, like other cultural artefacts, is subject to erosion with age; there must come a psychological moment after which states will tend not to defer to formulations which have gone unrenewed and unenforced for generations. Either the exercise of drafting and agreeing to international conventions has to be consistently repeated, or the existing conventions must be reinforced by a tradition of case law. The latter way of renewing them is better, since it enables the necessarily formal codification of the legal text to be given greater detail and flexibility from the encounter with concrete cases. Case law helps international conventions avoid abstractness, a fault which all too easily comes to mark the semi-idealised world of international law, which is capable of developing wholly speculative ideas such as the 'right to development'.[8] Furthermore, it can deal with changes as they arise. As

---

[8] Declaration on the Right to Development (1986), www.unhchr.ch; on which cf. Isabella Bunn, 'Legal and Moral Dimensions of the Right to Development', University of Bristol PhD thesis, 2001.

the aneurysm over aerial bombardment illustrates, the practice of war is a constantly changing thing and demands adaptability in the law that would govern it.

If it is practicable, then, we must devise a way of handling war crimes trials that will not be subject to the three objections we have noticed. Whether it is, in fact, practicable is something on which moralists are not qualified to pronounce, and on which they may be grateful to be excused from speculating. What a moralist can contribute to the enquiry, however, is a thought-experiment, a sketch of what a tribunal might look like that overcame the moral difficulties. And without saying whether the sketch is *practicable*, the moralist can and must be prepared to vouch for its being *realistic*. That is to say, it must presume no other moral relations than those which commonly obtain between human beings and human communities; it must not be predicated on a change in human nature, nor on the world's being in some important respect different from the way it is. We may sketch an ideal institution, but not an ideal world. Here, we may say, is what is realistically required; those who devise ways and means may tell us whether it could, in any circumstances, be given existence.

Let us embark upon our sketch, asking five questions: who should administer these tribunals? What kinds of cases should they hear? Who should be charged in them? What sanctions should they command? And when should cases be brought to trial?

(1) It is surely necessary to silence that cry of *Vae victis!* No tribunal will command authority unless the responsibility is taken out of the hands of belligerent powers and given to an internationally administered body. The International Committee of the Red Cross would doubtless find its humanitarian rôle compromised if it were to be entrusted with such a duty, but there must be scope for its rôle as guardian of the laws of war to be spun off upon a new Authority with a primarily inquisitorial mandate. The International Fact Finding Commission established in 1991 under the provisions of the First Geneva Protocol provides a foundation for this rôle. The idea of a standing court, however, has been entertained frequently in the UN

since the General Assembly proposed it in 1948.[9] The new body would need to be able to act continuously and on its own authority, warning belligerents of breaches of the law, and, where grave breaches were persisted in, establishing formal tribunals to deal with them. The occasional character of war crimes tribunals as we have known them so far tends to derogate from the authority of their judgments. They will never, we must hope, need to become frequent; but there must be some predictability about the decision-making that leads up to them, and this can only be achieved by entrusting it to a standing body.

(2) Two parallel and interdependent sets of documents and organisations have, in the second half of the twentieth century, championed the principles of *ius ad bellum* and *ius in bello* respectively; the United Nations Charter and Organization on the one hand, the Geneva Conventions and Protocols and the International Committee of the Red Cross on the other. This division of responsibility assigns the rôle of authorising and condemning resort to armed conflict to a body of diplomats and politicians. This is surely the right kind of court to decide this kind of question, in which so much depends on the reading of political circumstances and possibilities at a given time. A tribunal of lawyers, one must suspect, would have been out of its depth if asked to rule whether Croatia was justified in taking up arms against Yugoslavia in 1991. It would have become preoccupied with who fired the first shot, and when, and where, and it would have found it difficult to give proper weight to the complex constellation of political pressures which made the conflict seem reasonable, perhaps unavoidable, to those who embarked upon it. And its authority would have been weakened by the controversiality of its judgments, never to be forgotten or forgiven by those against whom its ruling fell. To say all this is not to acquiesce in the sceptical conclusion that *ius ad bellum* is absolutely unjusticiable. It is merely unjusticiable by

[9] The International Criminal Tribunal for the former Yugoslavia, created in May 1993 and located in The Hague, and the International Criminal Tribunal for Rwanda, established in November 1994 and sitting at Arusha, Tanzania, are the nearest approaches to it yet.

conventional judicial organs, but needs political organs that represent the world community at large. The strengthening of the UNO is the best means to bring the potential anarchy of *ius ad bellum* to some kind of order, calling on such sanctions as the Security Council can command: the armed resistance of the international community as a whole, and the likely prospect of defeat attending it.

With *ius in bello* it is quite a different matter. Within the terms laid down by a well-devised international law, such as I believe the First Geneva Protocol by and large to be, it is now possible for a nation to conduct armed struggle in a way that at least restrains the native inhumanity of war within more humane bounds. To judge breaches of these bounds is not a political task, and it is in everybody's interests, belligerent and non-belligerent, combatant and non-combatant, that they should be policed apolitically. The nineteenth-century argument that peace is served by enhancing the unbridled ferocity of war, an argument born of the marriage of scepticism and idealism, culminating in the stultifying nonsense of twentieth-century deterrence doctrine, should have lost its power to dazzle us by now. By implication the whole tradition of the law of war rejects it.[10] But here there is a major challenge to confront: how to include the actual conduct of hostilities within the scope of a tribunal. The tribunals of the forties administered a law that was weak in this area. Now that we have new provisions in place, tested by experience of conflict, the most urgent task is to make strategic crimes answerable to courts for the first time. Direct attacks on civilian populations or 'civilian objects', 'human-shield' tactics, deliberate destruction of cultural objects or of the environment, these are the matters, treated in Part IV Section I of the First Protocol, which any future war crimes tribunal must be able to prosecute effectively.

(3) Such matters of strategy cannot be dealt with unless the military and political leaders of the belligerent powers are liable to answer

---

[10] This was recognised by the government of France, which found in the submerged conflict between deterrence and the laws of war a sufficient reason not to give its signature to the First Geneva Protocol. Roberts & Guelff, *Documents*, pp. 464–5.

for the policies that they have ordered. But this must include the military and political leaders of the victorious party, even, in a conflict authorised by the Security Council itself, the military and political leaders of the law-enforcing party. It would be an outrage against equity to try bomber pilots and border guards if we could not try those who gave them their orders. But is that even thinkable?

One could imagine the inclusion in cease-fire agreements of an undertaking by both parties to give investigators from the War Crimes Authority access to records, and to facilitate the trial of its own political and military officers should the authority demand it. One could also imagine a convention whereby, if the Authority had had access during the conflict itself, no action would be made a subject of trial unless it had been the subject of a formal warning first, and had then been repeated. This would give some incentive to states to accept a monitoring oversight throughout hostilities and to avoid the embarrassment of trials later. But even so it would be difficult to achieve co-operation in the case of very senior figures in a régime, and the demand for trials could well encourage scapegoating to lower levels of responsibility. The arrest of Slobodan Milosevič in April 2001 and his subsequent extradition to The Hague came close to destabilising the new government of Yugoslavia.

And so, perhaps, some way would need to be devised by which a state could accept corporate responsibility for crimes committed in its name, trading a guilty plea for individual indemnities and negotiating penal damages. This would be less satisfactory from the point of view of justice, since it would enable those responsible to evade personal answerability, imposing the penalty instead upon the ordinary citizens, and especially the poor, in the form of economic hardship. But it might be preferable to have this option for co-operation than to have no co-operation at all. Here we touch upon the central practical problem of the whole enterprise: how to give nation-states an interest in furthering judicial processes which could be turned against themselves.

Should subordinates, too, be charged before an international tribunal? The course of justice as a whole would be much better served if they were made to answer to a domestic military law that had incorporated the principles of international law within it. This would go far to remove the problem of 'good faith'. If we intend that international law should be inter- rather than trans-national, then we must put the burden of mediating it upon the lawgivers of the nations, as the 1949 Geneva Conventions hoped would be the norm and, indeed, as has often been. The trial of minor figures before the Singapore tribunals presupposed not only the collapse of the Japanese régime but the total insufficiency of its law. It is not a good blueprint for an international order. Governments must be expected to incorporate the provisions of the law of war within their national codes. Failure to do so, or to enforce the provisions once incorporated, might be a suitable charge against senior officials to be heard by an international tribunal. Alternatively or as well, we could imagine the Authority requiring of a government that it should conduct its own trials of subordinates before international legal observers. And we can imagine changes to domestic military law being imposed upon a party in the terms of a cease-fire. But the more the responsibility for maintaining international law is thrust back on national governments and on their domestic laws, the more secure international law will become.

(4) The question about sanctions is really two questions: what punishments ought international tribunals to have at their disposal? and, what sanctions can the international community bring to bear to support the Authority in charge of them, and to ensure that rulings are complied with?

The tribunals of the forties sentenced some offenders to death. There can, in my view, be no objection to this in principle, given the nature of the offences in question. The usual norms of domestic justice in a civilised law-state increasingly tend to exclude the death penalty, and with good reason. But these reasons cannot be transferred without qualification to crimes committed in and by war, where the harm inflicted may be on such a monstrous scale. Imprisonment, too, is especially difficult to administer on an international basis and over a long period, as the gloomy last years of Rudolf Hess illustrated. Furthermore, when a conflict continues to run on or flares up again, the presence of prisoners is an incentive to renew hostilities, as, once again, the tragic recent history of Lebanon shows all too clearly. Death finishes the matter. It 'makes martyrs', perhaps, as the argument goes; but dead martyrs can sometimes have a positive political rôle, whereas living martyrs are a terrible liability.

However, the goal of war crimes tribunals cannot be to ensure that wicked people receive everything they have deserved, but simply to give effective and authoritative condemnation to a class of act hitherto supposed to be beyond public reprobation. We have to devise a symbolic language of punishment suited for precisely that end and no other. And the less extreme their impositions, the more probably they will secure essential co-operation. If international tribunals confine themselves, as I have suggested they should, to political and military leaders, it may be sufficient to arm them with just one penal power: disqualification from political or governmental office. To this we may, perhaps, add some ancillary disqualifications to prevent outrageous self-compensation: denial of government pension, of private profits of office, of passport, of the right to be party to an action in a foreign court, etc. The condemned person can then be handed over, as the excommunicate was handed over to the civil arm, for such further sanctions as domestic justice may impose on him.

But even the imposition of such penalties as these requires co-operation. If that co-operation is refused, what can the international community do about it? Nothing much, perhaps, short of renewing war (or economic sanctions, which ought to be seen as a form of war, subject to the same principles). The appalling prospect then opens up of an infinite series of self-fuelling conflicts. This may turn out to be the practical difficulty on which the whole enterprise is shipwrecked.

However, without being able to rule that worst possibility out, we may meet it with some observations that are slightly encouraging. No legal system can resist a concerted attempt to defy it. All law, whatever its sphere or provenance, survives on borrowed time – yet usually survives, nonetheless. Law receives its authority from government; the authority of government is based partly on power, partly on the recognition of the community, and partly upon that need for ordered justice which is instinctive in all human society. These elements are usually sufficient to keep some measure of authority and law in place. The occasional spectacular collapse reminds us of their fragility; but such calamities do not occur daily, because most people recognise their need for some government and some law. Those political orders are most successful which do not expect too much or offer too little, which afford appreciable protection but are not so demanding as to create a general interest in ignoring the law. And so it must be with international order too. There is a common interest in seeing the affairs of nations regulated lawfully. This interest can be made to serve the nascent international institutions if they are content to move by small and modest steps. There are a number of symbolic measures by which the international community shows disapproval of the rogues within its midst: eventually they affect the trading and political contacts available to the discredited party and tend, therefore, to be sufficiently disquieting to prompt adjustments of policy. These measures, perhaps formalised, will need to be enlisted in support of a War Crimes Authority. This will be done more easily if its rulings are not impossibly difficult for governments to comply with.

(5) We ask, finally, about the timing. No action can be judged satisfactorily years after the event. The ideal arrangement would be for the Authority to be involved in monitoring and information-gathering, and perhaps even in convening a tribunal, in the course of the hostilities themselves, enjoying access to both sides on the same basis as it is afforded to the Red Cross. But it is unlikely that this could always, or usually, be so. Quite apart from every belligerent's

natural tendency to defensiveness, there are good reasons of security that would make it inexpedient even for a well-intentioned state to facilitate the Authority's work in every respect while actively engaged in fighting. The best that can be hoped for, then, is some monitoring in the course of hostilities with a great deal of investigation afterwards.

There should, however, be a time-limit. The authority of justice depends on its success in *reacting* to offence. The reaction belongs within the same general context of action as the offence itself. Once that context has passed away and become the preserve of the historian, it is no longer possible to enter it again and act authentically within it. Where the limit should be set is indeterminate; it will always appear that you could have settled for six months less or six months more without making any difference. But we know it when we see the limit overstepped completely – as when we drag ex-Nazis from their bath-chairs in the geriatric wards and charge them with crimes committed fifty years ago.

Perhaps a theologian is likely to be especially conscious of the dangers of this proceeding, since he is aware how perilously placed the enterprise of human justice is as a whole. 'Judge not that you be not judged,' Christ taught us; and if our judgment is to serve any good at all, it must be conducted within the terms set by that warning 'judge not!'[11] The crimes committed by those elderly defendants may probably have merited severe punishment; the question is simply about our own competence to judge them. How can we understand what it was they did so long ago? How can we award them their deserts, having let our hands hang idle and the world move on for a whole half-century? The sudden zeal to tidy the matter up (before they should die peacefully in their beds!) is a piece of legal housekeeping worthy of Shakespeare's Angelo in *Measure for Measure*, that great theological protest against a jurisprudence that thinks it can settle absolutely everything. We who settle things are ourselves subject to settlement. Humility is the first condition for any humane justice.

[11] Matt. 7:1.

Only God has a right to carry justice to its limits, and, if he did, as Shakespeare asks us,

> How would you be
> If He, which is the tops of judgment, should
> But judge you as you are? O think on that;
> And mercy then will breathe within your lips
> Like man new made.[12]

And that is a lesson which must govern any project for extending the administration of law to new spheres of competence. Such a project tempts us to imagine that we can make our justice complete, as God's justice is complete. But how could any judgment by any court have expressed *all* that needed to be expressed about the bombing of Hiroshima, the massacre at My-Lai, or the destruction of Dubrovnik? All that a court can do is to set up a marker. The slow but real progress we have made towards a common understanding of what humanity in war requires of us makes some new markers necessary, simply to protect that gain in understanding. If we can set them up – and I hope we shall be able to – we must be sure to do it without pretentiousness.

---

[12] William Shakespeare, *Measure for Measure* 2.2.

6 | Afterword: without authority

In the memory of a life not over-stocked with drama a morning in January 1991 stands out, when my scheduled annual lecture series on the ethics of war opened just a few hours after the beginning of Operation Desert Storm for the liberation of Kuwait. An attendance several times the modest size usually expected for this subject shared the moment with me, and accompanied me through the term – until the military action ended before I did, when it fell away to more pacific pursuits. As the campaign proceeded, my habitual lectures were in need of daily rewriting, with new material for discussion thrust upon me by the unfolding events. It seemed as though the dream of the sixteenth-century fathers of 'just war' was in course of realisation as we talked about it: the conversion of bilateral conflict into an ordered exercise of third-party jurisdiction, enforced under international legal and moral norms.

The large attendance had its ludicrous aspect, conjuring up the picture of an earnest male student reaching for his textbook on sexual morality with his sweetheart already perched upon his knee, and shelving it again as she kissed goodbye. But it soon became apparent that Oxford students had no monopoly on a kind of absent-mindedness with respect to the great ethical issues of war and peace. The controversies that raged in the church and media before, during and after that military enterprise were at once furious and forgetful. I found myself in something of a minority in thinking that something excitingly new was transpiring. Everyone commented, of course, on the unprecedented impact of moment-by-moment media coverage; but how many noticed that the central topic of moral commentary, 'targeting', was one that had barely had a walk-on part in previous conflicts? And there were few enough even to reflect on the innovation of an international coalition in arms with the legal authorisation of the United Nations. The pack of moralists, breathlessly chasing the flow of information, seemed unaware of what most deserved their observation.

The year previously President Bush the elder had excited the universal mockery of the Euro-American intelligentsia with his remark about a 'new world order'. The only reason to mock the poor man, honestly, was the blinding obviousness of it. When a system of states built on the delicate balance of two superpowers and two ideologies was confronted with the collapse of one of them, there was going to be a new world order of *some* kind. But of what kind would that be? The Gulf War of 1991 offered one possible answer, a rather encouraging one: there could be an order in which international authority would play a decisive part in licensing the use of force, and international law would shape the conduct of military operations. Set free from the paralysis of cold-war years, the United Nations Organization looked ready for the part its founders had dreamed for it – to the discomfiture of some supporters who preferred it in its paralysed condition, morally inspiring and at a safe distance from the contamination of decisive action. The decade since then has seen other answers to the question, altogether less encouraging. The long and disfiguring tribal wars accompanying the disintegration of Yugoslavia showed that international paralysis was not a thing of the past. The poor continent of Africa had difficulty even in attracting attention for its spasms of horrific bloodletting. And which of all the hopes that were raised about *the* situation, Israel-Palestine, 'the marsh where the mosquitos breed' as Christopher Patten called it, has not proved illusory? The end is not yet. The promise of 1991 is still a promise.

Yet it is a promise not wholly belied. In November 2001, we were told, US commanders in Afghanistan went public with sharp criticism of their C in C, General Tommy Franks of US Central Command. Inviting opportunities to strike the enemy were being passed over, they complained, because, having reserved to itself the responsibility for clearing potential targets, Central Command was too cautious, too swayed by legal advisers, too concerned about the risk of hitting civilians. 'The whole issue of collateral damage . . . hamstrung the campaign.'[1] They may have had a point. Bureaucratic delay *can* compromise military effectiveness, caution over targeting *can* be misplaced. Yet, without having to decide the question at issue between General Franks and his subordinates, may we not derive encouragement from the fact that *this* is what military commanders now disagree about? What parallels could be produced from, let us say, the Second World War? The new orientation of military ethics to discriminate targeting seems to me a hugely important gain.

As I write, war between the west and Iraq is on the horizon again, and the virtues of the approach of 1991 become more apparent, even, perhaps, to those who had nothing good to say of it at the time. If the father chastised them with whips, the son has certainly chastised them with scorpions. Instead of a multilateral approach based on clear rulings of international authority, there has been feisty talk of unilateral action. Instead of a careful definition of just cause, there have been warnings of the peril of the world and a global indictment of an enemy whose name ends in '-ism'. Instead of war aims carefully drawn up in the light of the cause, 'régime change' has been declared as a goal even before the cause of war is clear. Now, I must disavow all knowledge of future events, being 'no prophet nor a prophet's son'; and as I write these words I have no foresight into whether, by the time they are read, there will be war against Iraq; and, if there is, what kind of a war, how authorised, with what participants, on what grounds and with what war aims. Nothing tells me whether it will, if it occurs, be a justified endeavour in any or all respects. Such a degree of ignorance, I am all too aware, makes me rather unusual, and puts me at an insuperable disadvantage not only in relation to

[1] Thomas Hicks and commentators, 'Target approval delays cost Air Force key hits', *Journal of Military Ethics* i(2), 2002, 109–35.

my future readers but to all the prephesic voices raised with perfect foreknowledge around me. But it does at least drive me back upon the deliberative posture of practical reasoning, for which the omniscient have no use. I am forced to consider how we may prepare ourselves to make right decisions as the need arises, rather than simply announce history beforehand.

Any private contribution to a current political debate must be, in Kierkegaard's phrase, 'without authority'. It is not in a position to make predictions. It is not in a position to make decisions. It is not even in a position to offer precise recommendations. Practical reasoning as such can only marshal reasons for decision as each new moment of decision arises; practical reasoning towards decisions that others must take can only clear the way for them to understand their responsibilities before God and their neighbours. Useful recommendations will tend to be introduced by the useful word, 'if'. That is to say, they will address *hypothetical* practical situations, not basing themselves on a pretended knowledge about what is, or what will be, the case.[2] 'Without authority', I can only *exemplify* the usefulness of the just-war proposal – by using it, as Paul Ramsey liked to say, 'as a tool to think with' about possible eventualities that are at the time of writing still stubbornly – and mercifully – hypothetical.

The long period of talking about, working up to, positioning around the project of a further Iraq war could have been an opportunity for churches to school their members, and all men and women of good will, in such an attitude, to rehearse them in *approaching* decisions that may need to be taken soon. The churches have shown themselves uninterested in doing this. Silent or dogmatic,

[2] The pioneering discussion, alas! universally ignored, of how churches can and cannot contribute usefully to public debates on war was that of Paul Ramsey, *Who Speaks for the Church?*, Nashville, Abingdon, 1967; Edinburgh, St Andrew, 1969. Ramsey took as a model for specific policy contributions his namesake Archbishop Michael Ramsey's advice to the British government in 1965: 'If [the Prime Minister] and his Government think it necessary to use force for the perpetuation of our existing obligations in Rhodesia, then a great body of Christan opinion in this country would support him in so doing.' See pp. 118–24.

or silently dogmatic and dogmatically silent, they have preferred, if they have uttered at all, to utter a *conclusion*, a bottom line to this and all possible future sums.

To illustrate the point, we may consider a document about which there are plenty of positive things to be said, that sent by the Bishops of the Church of England to the Commons Select Committee.[3] The six conclusions which this paper reaches are: that the policy of disarming Iraq of weapons of mass destruction is right; that the chief issue internationally is the authority of the UN; that this authority must be able to call upon military action in a last resort; but that 'a preventive war against Iraq' would be unacceptable 'at this juncture'; that the 'immense suffering' and 'unpredictable environmental, economic and political consequences' of war must be central to planning; and that the Middle East peace process must be revitalised. I find it hard to dissent from any of these. So, what is amiss? Simply, that they are not supported by any noticeable moral argument, instruction or guidance. The document professes 'the methodology associated with the just war tradition', but its *moral* content consists of no more than recommendations – *ex cathedra*.

There is, to be sure, a very informative *factual* content to the document. It contains a taut historical account of Iraq's intransigence in the face of the previous UN attempt to disarm it (6–18); a political analysis of American attitudes since 11 September 2001, and especially of the National Security Strategy document of September 2002 (19–33); a summary of the British government's recent assessment of Iraq's WMD capacity (34–44), and a survey of the Security Council Resolutions which comprise the legal basis for action against Iraq (45–9). Not matters, these, on which we expect our spiritual leaders to be so well informed, but it is welcome enough that they have taken expert advice on them. But just when we expect them to make use of

[3] *Evaluating the Threat of Military Action against Iraq: a submission by the House of Bishops to the House of Commons Foreign Affairs Select Committee's ongoing inquiry into the War on Terrorism*, 9 October 2002. The recommendations are at 1, repeated at 70.

this history lesson and exercise the authority of their spiritual teaching office, the sense of measured coherence which has marked the document so far suddenly disintegrates. A section curiously entitled 'the Church of England and Iraq' (50–69), is organised, even more curiously, under the headings, 'Jus ad bellum' and 'Jus in bello'. (What! Is the *Church of England* planning to make war on Iraq?) It consists of a disorganised patchwork of quotations from Bishops' speeches, reports of humanitarian visits, a critique of the US National Security Strategy, and then a whole series of alarms: alarms about the likely success of an invasion, alarms about the political prospects for Iraq after Saddam, alarms about Islamic–Christian relations, alarms about the degradation of the infrastructure of Iraq, alarms about Arab attitudes, alarms (even!) about the eventuality of a Kurdish state, alarms about anything, in fact, that might possibly be alarming in the prospect of war.

Three observations are in place, before we ask ourselves what kind of help the Bishops *might* have offered us.

(1) This, the Bishops' only statement so far on the prospect of war, is addressed to a House of Commons Select Committee. Our pastors have not thought it necessary to counsel *us* on how we should face our common responsibilities. The help that the just-war theory gives is, of course, meant for political leaders, not only for faithful private citizens. But it makes assumptions about the political leaders it addresses, namely, that they are either part of the Christian community or interested in understanding it, and in either case they need to know how the community of the faithful is to conceive *its* obligations in relation to Iraq. The Bishops may speak as authorised representatives *from* the Christian community *to* the state, or they may speak as pastors *to* the Christian community. But either way, the priority must be to communicate the *moral posture* of those who recognise their responsibilities for Iraq in Christ Jesus, rather than to dictate concrete policy conclusions, which, a month later, are already beginning to look out of date.

(2) The Bishops (and perhaps their advisers) found it easier to criticise the tendency of the US National Security Strategy towards the 'maintenance of a unipolar world', than to propose what was to be done in the matter of Iraq.[4] It is, of course, much *easier* to criticise America than to solve the problem of Iraq. The Western Alliance was beginning to creak ominously during President Clinton's administration, and under his inept successor the creakings, though temporarily eclipsed in the noise of 11 September 2001, have become steadily louder. Yet it would be wrong to place the blame for these strains wholly on one side. Brooding like a pregnant woman over the mighty future in her womb, Europe lays herself down on her cushions and scolds the boorish husband to whose attentions she looks for her comforts. 'Die USA und der Rest der Welt' is a melodrama that plays to packed houses throughout Europe; yet there is dishonesty in its perpetual hyperpower-angst.[5] As with the ten kings of John of Patmos's vision, who 'give up their power and authority to the beast' while turning in recrimination against the harlot who rides the beast, their resentment of Rome only another expression of dependence on imperial power, so it is with the European fascination with America.[6] By insisting that all the world's questions are in the end no more than a cover for the question of the Western Alliance, the only question worth asking, they give up their own sense of their responsibilities to the United States, and so make a beast out of it. Simply as a manner of proceeding, the Bishops would have done better to address the question of Iraq on its own terms first, and only then, when they had proposed something, ask to what extent the policies of the US administration were in accord.

(3) Expressions of alarm are no substitute for a serious attempt to weigh up the proportionate balance of harms in different courses of action and inaction. Of course, the prospects that reasonably alarm people must have their place in any judgment of proportion – but

---

[4] Ibid., 55

[5] The title of a recent book by Wilfried Röhrich. Münster, LitVerlag, 2002.

[6] Rev. 17:13–18.

'the methodology associated with the just war tradition' is actually to *weigh* these against one another, not simply to pile them up. The extent to which weighing is possible is usually limited, and so 'the methodology associated with the just war tradition' also requires of us a good sense of the limitations of our prudence, which is to say, faith and courage. It would be embarrassing to rehearse today all the desperate predictions that were made by churchmen in 1990–1 about the outcome of engaging with Iraq. That does not mean that it was unreasonable to have such anxieties at that point. It means only that having reasonable anxieties is one thing, making a well-informed prudential judgment on the consequences of what one does is something quite different. Being hypnotised by terrors in one direction while failing to notice terrors in other directions is not prudence, nor anything like it. The methodology associated with the just-war tradition also implies distinguishing the part played by public debate from the part played by executive decision. Ramsey used to emphasise that prudential calculations are hardly amenable to public debate, whereas the principle of discrimination is something that a conscientiously reflective public can reasonably and intelligently press upon its military and political leaders. On that principle, however, the Bishops astonishingly have nothing to say.

The position the Bishops have taken – which, as I say, commands my own sympathies – is grounded in a moral argument that they were not prepared to expose more than very fragmentarily. This concerns two possible forms in which the 'just cause' criterion might be met, one currently represented by the strategic thinking of the US government, the other by that of the British government. The one envisages a primarily *defensive* war, the other a primarily *penal* war. Had the Bishops exposed their argument, they would have said: for a cause to be just, it must be based not simply on the peril that Iraq's weapons pose to the world, but on a need to vindicate decisively the judgments of the United Nations Security Council. They did not expose this argument, because they did not wish to *appear* to be in favour of war against Iraq on any ground whatever. Yet they are in favour of war against Iraq on one possible ground. That is the logic of two assertions which appear in their recommendations, that 'the primary international concern remains Iraq's blatant disregard of the UN and of its authority', and that 'in those instances where diplomatic and economic pressure fail to ensure compliance with UNSC resolutions, military action can sometimes be justified as a last resort to enforce those resolutions'.

It is the great temptation of church leaders to try to *conceal* the fact when they do, in truth, support resort to armed conflict, however reluctantly, on certain possible grounds. (The phrase 'as a last resort' serves as a useful device of concealment when it means, 'in some not impossible circumstances which it is not expedient for us to explain now'.) The logic of deploring war is simple and inexorable; and it is time that church leaders learned it. If they proceed *purely negatively*, crying down recourse to arms for this or another cause, they drive the whole weight of justification back upon the plea of *defence*; and this produces the aneurysm in the defensive rationale, the sprawling suburbs of Article 51, which have been the hallmark of too much twentieth-century justification of war. If, on the other hand, they proceed *positively*, by crying up the authority of international tribunals of judgment, they divert the justification of armed conflict into a primarily *penal* matrix, since the final ground for military action will then always be the vindication of international authority against defiance. (It is necessary to say 'primarily', because the other causes are not simply absent: a *sufficient* wrong in need of reparation, a *sufficient* peril in not repairing it, will still be necessary conditions for thinking it important enough to vindicate authority in this case.)

The US emphasis on preventive war follows faithfully the dominant twentieth-century line of moralising. When the Bishops declare, rather pompously, that 'the US National Security Strategy and its application to Iraq are matters of grave concern to the church', one is tempted to comment that they certainly should be, since they count

Lambeth 1930 and John XXIII among their intellectual progenitors![7] There is in the US document, of course, a tendency to stretch the boundaries of *immediate* peril to allow a more extensive defensive ground for pre-emptive strike. But such a development is inevitable, as I have argued above, if other just causes must be represented as though they were simply defensive.

The Bishops handle the question of pre-emption rather well, reinforcing the Grotian judgment that 'the danger must be immediate . . . those who accept fear of any sort as a justification for preemptive slaughter are themselves greatly deceived and deceive others'.[8] Their move towards the recovery of penal cause, moreover, admirably reflects the Christian instinct that the essential form of justified armed conflict is judgment, that the best form of judgment is the declaration of a third-party authority, and that armed conflict can only be a possibility in reserve for when authority is reduced to impotence. Yet the gains that they have won from this reorientation of just cause seem to be thrown away, because they will not articulate the real logic of their thought. Their negative recommendation about defensive war ends up significantly qualified: 'to undertake a preventive war against Iraq *at this juncture* would be to lower the threshold for war unacceptably'. The words which I emphasise could, I suppose, be given a favourable reading, to mean 'before there has been a decisive attempt to bring the Iraq government into compliance with Security Council authority'. But if they meant that, the war would not be a *preventive* war, strictly speaking, at all. That the words 'at this juncture' should not be redundant, one must take them to mean, 'before the danger is more immediate than it now is'. In which case, the Bishops have not finally refocussed the just cause after all. They have left us with

---

[7] *Evaluating the Threat*, 56.

[8] *De iure belli ac pacis* 2.1.5, which the Bishops do not quote (eds, B.J.A. de Kanter-van Hettinga Tromp, R. Feenstra and C.E. Persenaire, Aalen, Germany, Scientia Verlag, 1993, p. 172). At *Evaluating the Threat*, 54 the view is attributed on secondary authority to Augustine and Aquinas, implausibly.

a primarily preventive cause for war, objecting to acting on it at this moment merely on the grounds that the danger is not *yet* immediate *enough*. But just how immediate the danger presently is, is not the kind of thing that Bishops are paid, or trained, to tell us. We all know that they know no more about it than the rest of us, and that what is said upon such a subject today may be out of date tomorrow. What they *might* have known about, but have *not* in this case told us, is *whether a purely preventive cause for war is ever valid in any degree of urgency whatever.*

My own approach to this question I have laid out above: all actually justified resorts to war combine, in some measure, all the three traditional causes: defence, reparation and punishment. To that I now add the following observation: to the extent that one takes international authority seriously, one treats the penal cause as the *presenting* cause. *The decisive point* in the crystallising of cause for war is that international authority must be vindicated. But this does not mean that international authority may command a war to vindicate itself without substantial *underlying* causes of other kinds. As one should not be sent to jail for contempt of court for blowing one's nose while the judge is talking, so a nation should not be condemned to war for failing to implement a Security Council Resolution on which nothing of great weight hangs. A defensive cause in general terms will be a feature of every decision to take up arms, for here the question of discriminate cause fades off into the question of proportionate cause: without some grave danger from *not* going to war, the danger *of* going to war will always be unwarranted. But a defensive cause in particular terms, too, may also be a major element. It would not be wrong, for example, for the Security Council to resort to armed conflict if its authority had consistently failed to restrain a power from accumulating weapons of mass destruction – and to avoid the wretched ambiguities over nuclear weapons, let us say, quite precisely, biological weapons prohibited by international treaty and designed for use against populations. And here we need not resist in principle the proposal of the US National Security Strategy document to 'adapt the concept of imminent threat to the capabilities and objectives of today's adversaries'. That need only mean that the meaning of 'imminent' is context-dependent and content-dependent, which is ordinary common sense. The threat must be real, certain, and evidently ineluctable; but nobody has to put a time-limit upon it, so as to say, for example, that one may attack an enemy if one expects it to attack within twenty-four hours, but not if one expects it to attack within twenty-four days. And the more terrible the threat, the more 'imminent' it becomes. The prospect of a massive counter-population biological attack in twenty-four days' time may justify going to war without delay, whereas the prospect of a limited troop invasion may still invite a week or two's further haggling at the table.

But could a peril become so imminent as to be the *presenting* cause, as well as the *underlying* cause, of resort to war? Yes, obviously it could; but only if the urgency were such as to make further action by international authority impossible. And here we conclude with a point of great importance, not only for the ethics of war but for the ethics of civil justice, too: the duty of deferring to governmental authority is dependent on the availability of that authority and its capacity to act decisively in a crisis. Just as private citizens may tackle and detain a mugger in the absence of the police, improvising a form of government where the official form is not at hand, so a nation may improvise international justice where international authority is not capable of enacting it. If defence becomes the presenting cause, that implies that international authority has lost effective control of events, has, as it were, ceased to exist as a *practical* factor in the situation.

Much of the tension between the USA and the other members of the Security Council in recent months had to do with the likely effectiveness of what was called, none too respectfully, 'the UN route'. The USA has to bear its own share of responsibility for weakening the authority of that body; yet the concern was not unreasonable in itself. Those who believe in the importance of international authority must understand that authority can be retained only by effective decision and action. The quickest way to make the great UN experiment a memory of past history is to try to use it as an icepack to freeze the nations of the world into inactivity. In civil society the authority of courts is diminished if access to them is costly and slow, if their procedures are cumbrous and their arguments unnecessarily prolonged. So it will be with this international tribunal: it will become weaker, the more irresolute and inconclusive its proceedings are. Unfortunately, there are legal practitioners who mistakenly suppose that each additional argument, each new deferral somehow adorns the majesty of the law. And the United Nations Organization has its lovers who view any indication of action on its part as sad confirmation that it has been somehow been taken over by US interests. But the UN was not devised as a temple of contemplation, but as a giver of law for international action. The crucial and still unsolved question about the future of war as such is whether the UN can be shaped to act with reliable effectiveness.

It would, of course, have been a disgrace for the USA not to go to the UN over the Iraq crisis; and it will be a disgrace if the USA does not return there, should the UN's authority be flouted further. But it would have been worse than a disgrace; it would have been a self-destructive abnegation of authority, had the UN failed, when the USA came to it, to grasp the challenge of giving law decisively in the crisis. As I write these words in Advent 2002, with 'men fainting with fear and with foreboding of what is coming on the world', this latest provision of God's common grace has so far not failed to give its law. I pray that it may not have failed by the time the reader ponders what I write. If it has, 'look up and raise your heads, because your redemption is drawing near'.[9] Yet it may still be that the end is not yet. For while God restrains his coming, there will be provisions of his common grace; and these may have to serve one more turn before our King comes to us.

[9] Matt. 24:6; Luke 21:26, 28.

Index